THE FLOWERING OF MANAGEMENT

THE FLOWERING OF
MANAGEMENT

Pravir Malik

SRI AUROBINDO INSTITUTE OF
RESEARCH IN SOCIAL SCIENCES
SRI AUROBINDO SOCIETY
PONDICHERRY - 605002

First Edition: February 1997

(Typeset in 10.5/12.5 pt. Times New Roman)

ISBN 81-7060-106-1

Copyright Pravir Malik and Sri Aurobindo Society 1997
Published by Sri Aurobindo Institute of Research in Social Sciences,
A Unit of Sri Aurobindo Society, Pondicherry - 605 002
Printed at Sri Aurobindo Ashram Press, Pondicherry - 605 002
PRINTED IN INDIA

What now we see is a shadow of what must come.

Savitri, *Sri Aurobindo*

CONTENTS

CONTENTS

PREFACE

The Flowering of Management is about the change in management consciousness that must occur if our organizations are to be managed more effectively and in consonance with the deeper laws of being. Chapter 1 emphasizes the need for change, especially in light of the overwhelming materialistic development that is taking place on a global level. Chapter 2 points out that this change has in fact already begun and is causing organizations to refocus their attention at the level of the individual. Chapter 3 discusses common business ignorances which when addressed will align the organization with these deeper forces for development. Chapter 4 presents a method for predicting which of the myriad of recently emerging management panaceas will endure. Chapter 5 discusses the inherent human resistance to change and how this may be overcome. Chapters 6 and 7 present key societal enablers which when mobilized can further assist in ushering in the individual and organizational change in management consciousness. Chapter 8 suggests altering the definition of profit to better align organizations with the goals of Nature. Chapter 9 places the imminent change in consciousness in perspective by indicating where in the overall scheme it lies. A postscript chapter, 'Dynamization of a Synthesized World Current,' suggests a means by which management change can be made more pervasive and puissant.

Though these chapters are arranged so as to develop the underlying theme of change in management consciousness, they may be read in any order as each chapter has been written to stand as a separate whole.

PRAVIR MALIK, EVANSTON, 1996.

ACKNOWLEDGMENTS

The Flowering of Management is a collection of articles which have been written during the last two years. Several people have reviewed many of these articles and have provided constructive feedback. Others have provided constant encouragement. My sincere thanks to R.Y. Deshpande, Akash Deshpande, Tara Jauhar, Luc and Suzie Venet, Vasant Merchant, Harish & Rani Malik, Debashish Banerji, Nirankar Agarwal, Kailash Jhaveri, Dimple Uberoi, Chitvan Malik, M.S. Srinivasan, and Vijay for their feedback and constant encouragement.

Several of the articles have previously appeared in Mother India and International Journal of Humanities and Peace and I would like to thankfully acknowledge their respective editors and publishers for allowing these articles to be reprinted here. "The Inward Movement" appeared as "Evolution of Consulting" in the September 1994 issue of Mother India. "Money" appeared in the May 1996 issue of Mother India. "Rethinking Business Basics" appeared as "Aligning Businesses to Achieve World Peace" in the 1995 issue of International Journal of Humanities and Peace. "The New Paradigm" appeared in the 1996 issue of International Journal of Humanities and Peace.

I would also like to acknowledge that the ideas pertaining to physics and design science have been developed through studying the works of R. Buckminster Fuller. Curious readers may contact the Buckminster Fuller Institute, Santa Barbara, USA, for more details.

I also express my thanks to Sri Aurobindo Society for

publishing The Flowering of Management, and to Auro-Soorya, Amravan, Konark Aviation, and Designer Holidays for financing its publishing.

Finally, I express my profound gratitude to Sri Aurobindo and The Mother for enfolding me in Their Reality and for providing the comprehensive background and integral view of life which forms the foundation for these articles. Interested readers are referred to The Collected Works of Sri Aurobindo, and The Collected Works of The Mother, both published by Sri Aurobindo Ashram, Pondicherry, India, for more details.

INTRODUCTION

The world is going through an increasingly rapid development. More powerful and enabling technologies are constantly being created. Life and its choices are becoming more complex. Yet the innate ability of human beings has remained the same. Mind is still used as the primary problem-solving tool and as the growing number of prevailing problems in individual, organizational, societal, political, economical, and environmental spheres will attest to, has been unable to sufficiently solve them. These two movements - the rapid materialistic progress multiplying choices and the complexity of life, and a boiling up of the numerous problems in every sphere of life - necessitate that man alter radically his view of himself and the world and his functioning as a being in order that the problems may begin to be adequately solved. A new manager able to function in a radically different manner is the requirement of today. Chapter 1, "The New Manager," expands on this basic theme.

Whilst these two movements may indicate that man is being prepared for some other mode of operation, certain universal trends dealt with in Chapter 2, "The Inward Movement," will more aptly point out that indeed this is the case. There has been an inward-focused movement with a settling on the individual, with its consequent need of his integral development, as the culminating step. In this rapidly changing global environment organizations need to rethink the way they do business and manage themselves. Chapter 3, "Rethinking Business Basics," examines seven ways in which businesses can change the way they function to harmonize their functioning and development with the movements and trends that are occurring at a global level. In the bargain, since they will be operating from a more complete and thorough perspective, they will boost their own chances of success.

A number of new managerial panaceas to deal with the rapidly changing, and increasingly complex global environment have arisen recently. Yet not all of these will be successful. Chapter 4, "Predicting Successful Management Practice," offers a method by which success may be predicted by drawing insight from paradigms in other fields of experience - namely, 'Quantum physics' and 'A realized human's experience of life'. The latter paradigm is in fact isolated as being the driver of all other paradigms and prediction linked to it is positioned as being the most accurate.

While organizations have been strategizing and reengineering to become more efficient and effective in the global environment, and while they have even taken consideration of their core assets, people, in the implementation of plans, they still rarely succeed, or succeed only with difficulty because they have not delved deeply enough into the nature of people. Chapter 5, "Change Management," considers a deeper approach to dealing with and overcoming the inherent resistance in people, so that companies can realize their plans effectively, efficiently, and fully.

The changes that are occurring require companies and organizations to rethink the way they function in light of the ideas presented in the preceding chapters. Yet there are two crucial ingredients - Money and Education which must be mobilized in the spirit consistent with what is to be achieved to proactively shape the future. Chapter 6, "Money," delves into the nature in which money is currently being used, its associated problems, and why it is being used in this manner. It also suggests alternative uses of money aimed at developing the consciousness of people and of humanity. Chapter 7, "Education," suggests ways that businesses can help with our one most important asset, children, in solving Earth's current problems and developing a future harmonious environment. The goals of education are first set out, and then ways are suggested in which businesses can offer long-term help in light of these goals.

Chapter 8, "Towards Comprehensive Business Efficiency," examines the much highlighted principle of 'profit', and concurs that while its consideration is essential in achieving the efficiency inherent in all Nature's constructs, yet its definition is incomplete and needs to be enhanced to include alignment with Nature's goals. Chapter 9, "The New Paradigm," takes a penetrating look at our current management systems. It isolates where on the spectrum of consciousness these systems of management lie, and suggests where they are leading to, in light of the stage of evolution which is revealing itself as active now.

A postscript chapter, "Dynamization of a Synthesized World Current", examines a method by which the force of spirituality, relatively dormant vis-à-vis the force of materiality, can be strengthened so as to create a more puissant synthesis, globe-encompassing in its effects, of the two movements of Nature.

CHAPTER 1

THE NEW MANAGER

Our lives are changing at an increasingly rapid pace. Man is able to explore the universes around him, is able to probe the complexity of the atom, and is able to prepare substances that assist in alleviating physical discomfort and disease. Technology has dissolved barriers between parts of the world and while some centuries ago exploration required that a band of men set sail across the seas to physically discover other parts of the world, exploration today requires simply that one have access to the Internet. Man's very life has been enriched a thousand-fold. He has easy access to foods from around the world, he has access to and can indulge in various forms of entertainment, and he has access to goods of all kinds which add comfort and luxury to his life and existence. His basic capability as a being, however, has remained unchanged.

Regardless of complexity, situations are still dealt with in a simple manner. Consider, for example, the much debated issue of abortion. Man would like one simple law to dictate whether abortion is illegal or legal. Those who would illegalize it claim that life must be preserved at any cost. Regardless of the circumstances of pregnancy, and regardless of the stability of the parents, or of the environment in which the child is to be brought up, life must be protected since it is a gift from God. Pro-choice advocates claim that the choice to have a child must be the parents', since it is their child and their life that is being affected, and therefore they alone can and must have the final say in whether their child is to be born or not.

Both these arguments are overly simple and operate on a foundation of man-made morality. Yet morality is relative and differs not only across two separate eras in time, but even across two places in the same era. Behavior dictated by man-made morality may have been adequate in past history, when development proceeded along a more defined line and every issue was more clearly black or white. In today's complex environment, where a more intricate and subtle balance is being worked out between the individual and the collective, however, man-made rules based on his inaccurate and incomplete rendering of reality prove vastly inadequate. Man in his present state is bound to be confused by a situation in which complex choice exists, because he is not viewing the picture completely or accurately. Man assumes that life begins where birth takes place and ends where death takes place. He assumes that reality is described by what his physical organs perceive.

His approach to life is entirely one-dimensional. It is a linear progression with beginning, end, and journey mapped by what the senses are able to perceive. This single-dimensional approach is a good first approximation and may have been more appropriate in a world where complexity and variety were still more latent. Today, complexity and variety are the very status and norm of life, and to cope more completely man has to leap from his childish grappling with the environment to a mature and many-sided comprehension and understanding of its realities. If, for example, it is assumed that life always exists and that birth and death are just stages in its progression, then the playing field, as it were, is at once enlarged to scan eternity. For birth and death are not then the beginning and end, but merely events in a drawn-out progression which has been in existence since eons before and continues unendingly into some possibly unforeseeable future. If it is further assumed that each life is a thread or movement initiated to fulfill some intention, and that the interplay of lives too are architectured to push forward that intention, then we open ourselves to possibilities and functionings which take on a supra-terrestrial significance.

In the above example, therefore, it may be the case that in spite of her extreme poverty, the mother must bare the child, so that both she and the child are chiseled by the secret intention to become more noble and enduring. Just as possible, it may be the case that the fetus is to be terminated so that people associated with the parents and they themselves may awaken to a deeper questioning and to a truer meaning of life and death. The point is, given our current abilities and perceptions it may be impossible to know what really is to be done. The more correct thing to be done exists, but if we are unable to perceive the whole situation and accurately determine what is best for all involved and in line with the secret intention, how truly, can we make a right decision? Man attempts to create a single law to deal with complex situations whose outcome really, should vary according to the particular circumstance. The increasing complexity in our world has arisen so that man can forgo his petty mentality and narrow perception and know and do what is in consonance with the whole truth and the secret intention.

In management, a different kind of manager is needed. The manager of today uses his mind to map out possibilities to the best of his ability, oftentimes only to then arbitrarily decide, based on some feeling, the sources of which he is unaware of, or on some motive operating within his being which may have nothing to do with the problem at hand, or in the best case, on the calculated best returns from his mapped and most probably incomplete set of possibilities, on a path of action. The nature of mind however, the chief tool of the manager, is to divide. It can deal with problems only by breaking them up into components and then seizing on one component in preference to another. This inability of the mind is superimposed upon the mass of desires, likes, dislikes, biases which are already ingrained in the being and exercise their covert and even overt influence, to thereby further enervate the manager's ability to make a holistic decision in harmony with the secret intentions of nature.

The result is the chaos we see around us today. If this method of problem-solving had merit to it, our social, political, economic, environmental, and personal realities would be other than they are today. Instead, skin color is still an issue amongst people, races fight others in order to cleanse their life of lesser mortals, religions claim to be the whole and only truth thus entrapping their cohorts in rigid and unhealthy worlds, money meant for social development is usurped by politicians, people are coerced into voting for one asura, or another, corruption and bribery run rampant from the top echelons down to blue collar levels, developed countries dump their toxic goods in the third world, and economists don't understand what money is and construct policies which end up completely counteracting their original intention.

The list of maladies is endless. Clearly, if man's current capacities, abilities, and view of situations were accurate and true, none of these circumstances would be proceeding in the manner they are proceeding in today. One doesn't have to tread very far to observe that something is not quite right. Each person is himself afflicted with numerous tensions, anxieties, disturbances, fears, compulsive thoughts, physical illnesses, that are part of his being and existence. If man had the right view and the right knowledge, why would such situations continue to exist? He has created medicine to fight depression. When taken over years it brings to him instead cancers or heart disease. His medicines for heart disease give him perpetual diarrhea, and medicines for diarrhea give him in return depression. Man is caught in similar self-defeating circles in every sphere of his life because he does not understand who he is, or what life is. Man must awaken to his incapacity and realize that what he thought to be true obviously is not. The management of self, environment, politics, society, organizations, is inadequate. And this is no surprise since man operates within an artificial single-dimensional playing field, and uses mentality as his chief instrument.

Yet the 21st century is approaching. The outer world will continue to become more complex. The vast amounts of information, the vast number of choices, the number of possibilities which must be managed necessitates a change in consciousness in man. They necessitate his leaping into unknown dimensions and developing more comprehensive tools, other than mentality, to master his environment, to understand the hidden forces and intentions at work, and most importantly to understand and master first his own nature, without which nothing else can be mastered.

There are two principles at work whose significance when understood indicate that man is being made ready for some other mode of operation. There is a first indication, manifest as the significant material progress, as to the future man may be party too. There is also a pressure from around forcing to the surface all that must be altered in man's nature, his actions, and his works. Information and knowledge technology, transportational efficiency, architectural prowess, medical breakthroughs, are a first approximation of the power and ability that shall manifest at the level of matter. But at the same time the individual and societal grooves that spiral and criss-cross to form a rock-like and impenetrable structure, to offer a basis for life to manifest on, must itself be altered so that yesterday's patterns, beliefs, tendencies, outlooks are replaced by a more supple, plastic, and fluid basis. All one's inertia must dissolve and give way to another way of being.

Man had been in a slumber and only now is beginning to awake from it. The progress of matter facilitates this process of awakening. The imagination and the dream-ability of humans gets ignited. For now we can probe the infinitesimal world of the atom, can extend our observation to the far reaches of distant galaxies, can communicate instantaneously with others on the far side of the globe, can accurately observe and predict weather patterns and minute movements all over Earth from satellites in the skies, can beautifully capture the messages and essence of many aspects of life and many personalities on film, can harness energy from the sun, can construct architectural master-pieces which rise unendingly towards the sky, and cram computing power onto a chip the size of a thumb-nail. Such realities ignite us to dream and aspire for the impossible. But also it shows us that what may have been but a glimmer in the eye of some mind can indeed be made real. All these breath-taking developments are signs and sureties of the possibilities that man is awakening to. We are becoming or can become conscious collaborators in the destiny of Earth.

But before that happens, the other movement which is now in effect, and manifest as the various personal, environmental, societal problems, to mention a few, must be heeded and mastered. All the fears, anxieties, destructive thoughts, limiting thoughts, prejudices, biases, inertia, anger, that we are prone to, that are ingrained within us, must be removed, altered, completely overcome, if the dreams and possibilities are to be realized. This movement has grown in force and urgency. The primary concerns of many have shifted to their personal lives and this has to be if indeed man is to transcend his present status of being. The concerns a century ago may have been more with national independence, with the building of infrastructure, with the development of communities and other macro-level issues. While that is still a concern, attention on the micro-level, on our own natures, has become more urgent and the focus of today. And yet without a doubt, once some mastery has been achieved at the micro-level, or at least once it has become easier to place attention at the level of the individual to better understand why and how he functions and who he really is, as surely as the sun rises each day, we shall spiral back from a more conscious vantage point to view and consider again the larger, more macro-level workings of life.

The manager of yesterday has operated within a framework in which materialistic development propelled mainly by commercial considerations has been the scope of his functioning. This framework must alter and life must be looked at anew from a more comprehensive angle, to offer the possibility of a more puissant and effective action in the management of tomorrow. A lack of consideration of what is happening within and around us and why it is happening cannot lead to effective decision-making and effective action. The manager of tomorrow must become a center through which world-energies can act effectively and achieve their purpose. But for this to happen the consciousness of managers has itself to go through a change so that the larger movements and secret and inevitable intentions of nature may be rightly recognized and consequently more smoothly fulfilled.

Chapter 2

THE INWARD MOVEMENT

From separate and continuously forming nations scattered across the globe, barely aware of one another's existence, and with local inhabitants perceiving all reality as only what the eye can see, we have reached a stage in evolution where international boundaries are crumbling and the world is fast becoming a truly integrated and global village. Change is taking place at an accelerated pace, and regardless of the line of practicality we pursue, whether scientific, geographic, or economic, the same trend manifests itself. There is a movement to search within, a movement to discover what lies at the core, a movement which culminates in the revelation of the innate interconnectedness and 'oneness' of all things.

Consider physics. In the search for discovering the truth of phenomena, of why an action gives rise to an opposite and equal reaction, or of why a flower is yellow, scientists have been lead into the world of atoms. From the classical view of an atom being the indestructible and isolated building block of the universe, physicists have arrived at the quantum view of the fundamental wave-particle, which is neither here nor there, and yet everywhere, and which is intricately connected to all wave-particles everywhere else. The search lead within, and then to a vast 'oneness' made apparent through the interconnectedness.

Consider geography. The explanation of winds, the finding of fish skeleton in the sky-reaching Himalayas, have lead geographers to try to understand core causal agents such as the sun and tectonic plates. All visible geographic phenomenon is now explained in terms of these few fundamental agents - the 'wave-particles' if you will, of geography. Further, it has been found that an act or phenomenon occurring in one part of the world intimately affects what happens elsewhere. Hypothetically, a mere leaf falling off a tree in the Amazon forest can conceivably create a minute stir in the air which can create a larger stir, and so on, which can ultimately manifest as a wind on the Siberian planes. As in physics, geographic phenomenon too has been explained in terms of certain core agents, which it has been found have a universal coverage.

Consider finance. The financial health of an economy until quite recently, would be determined through the sole scrutiny of a few fundamental variables such as interest rates, exchange rates, amongst others. Today, such fundamental phenomena as the weather, and its effect on doing business, the health of a president, and the number of university graduates, are considered in determining the financial health of an economy. Furthermore, the falling ill of the president in USA say, can cause the Dow Jones in New York to fluctuate substantially, consequently sending ripples of concern through all the stock-markets of the world. Again, there has been a movement to understand the financial situation in terms of core components, and in terms of the vast interconnectedness of phenomena.

How do these trends which are taking place universally, show up in management? Or is the management world an instance where this does not occur? I contend that there are no exceptions, and an understanding of what has been at the forefront of management thought and what is today at the forefront of management thought will reveal the same universal trend, and thereby reveal the direction and the future of the management world. For the purpose of discussion, the trend and the future of the management world can be considered as two separate issues. Let us first consider the trend, and once that has become clear, then consider the future that this trend leads into.

Organizations function within a certain societal framework. In making decisions on what they will produce, how they will produce it, who they will produce it for, and why they will produce it, they of necessity must consider their competition, their own state, and what the needs of society are. They must consider such high-level variables as interest rates, inflation rates, exchange rates amongst others, in making an informed decision. In addition, they must consider market-based variables, such as market share, market growth, costs of producing goods, potential sales and others. These variables and associated modes of attention fall under the general province of strategy, an area which has received much attention in recent times. Entire companies have arisen to conceive and plan strategies for other companies so that they may perform effectively in the increasingly complex world of today.

More recently reengineering has grown in importance, and has become the focal point of attention and the arena for the further creation of several companies. Reengineering is concerned with better organizing the way a company does business, by focusing directly on the customer value-creating processes companies are involved in. Unlike strategy where the concerns are primarily external, and where a company is trying to arrive at a position which will allow it to masterfully maneuver through a play of external forces, reengineering is more inward focused and aims at providing an equilibrium between internal and external forces by aligning the internal with the external, consequently allowing a company to sustain a positive position with respect to its environment. In that this approach is aimed at aligning the organization with the intricate complexities of the environment, it has the same relationship to strategy as teaching a poor man to grow oranges has to giving a poor man oranges to eat. In that giving a poor man oranges to eat will only feed him for a day, strategy in isolation, will only suggest a solution temporary and immediate in its reach. In that teaching a poor man to grow oranges provides him with food for a season, reengineering, through aligning the organization with currently existing realities, provides an organization with the ability to respond in real-time to a series of thrusts, influences, and opportunities, focused on it from the outside.

But what when current realities are subject to change? How long will this current reality, which reengineering provides a company ammunition for, hold-up? How long will the forces that rest in this temporary grimace we see and experience now, hold up before swirling into another reality radically different from the one we are in now? Today's world, as is apparent from the vast array of changes constantly occurring, is only a melting pot for influences and tendencies initiated as long as centuries ago. Black moves toward white, and big toward small, languages coalesce, and thoughts of unity and universal harmony ring through the minds of many. But none of this has yet happened. And that is the whole point. The externalities today are a stance the many forces have assumed in their dynamic dance toward their goal. How long this current equilibrium will be held before those very forces impelled by their age-old impulses, decide that it is time to move on toward the next stance is the crucial question.

Where does this outward-looking strategy aimed at providing oranges for a day that has given way to the more inward-looking reengineering aimed at providing oranges for a season, end? What will be the next step in the decision-making which is playing such an important role in the formation of our businesses and consequently in their impact on individuals and the evolution of society? In that an individual lies at the center of an organization, and in that the trend has been from out to in, by the very momentum built into trends and by the fact that trends have a tendency to complete the intention they were initiated to complete, the next focal point and crux of decision-making will be at the level of the individual himself. And in that Nature insists there be an inward-looking trend, as made apparent by the many contemporary universal trends, those companies that carry that inward motion to its conclusion shall be the one's rewarded, while those that focus solely on the external without regard to the inner realities and necessities, will find it more and more difficult to continue doing profitable business in that manner, if for no other reason than that the content of their solutions and suggestions will continually be of a sub-optimal standard because of the lack of consideration of root causes.

Strategy can be looked at as the flavor and appearance of a cake; reengineering as the cake; and the utensils, methodology and ingredients by which the cake has been made, as the focus of the next phase in management. Let us refer to this phase as "Individualization". It is that realm where all Nature is pointing us towards, and where our future survival and growth as humans, as companies, and as a World, will issue from. All that is built around us is through the power of the individual. It is only in completely understanding him, just as we do the mechanics of increasing market share, or of building viable business processes, and then harnessing that understanding, that we may further build into realms that seem impossible now. It is only in getting at the root of the intelligence and power and harmony and capacity for organization inherent within individuals that we can make that step which Nature is demanding of us.

Just as strategy is the masterful maneuvering of a company through external forces, and reengineering is the balance of internal forces through alignment with external forces, individualization is the dynamic balance of internal forces so that it is always aligned with external forces as and when they change. If strategy is giving a man oranges to eat to thereby feed him for a day, and reengineering is teaching a man to grow oranges to thereby feed him for a season, individualization is teaching a man to grow foods depending on the season, to thereby feed him for a lifetime. If we accept this trend as true then we can hypothesize that those companies that fulfill the trend will be rewarded.

Companies that practice pure strategy may continue to exist; but of necessity strategy as implied today will be only a phase, the flavor of a cake, in any company decision-making or business decision implementation process. Value will be added through reengineering, and even more value will be added through individualization. A company requiring traditional strategy work, must have its individualization and reengineering work complete, in order for the strategy to be effective and far-lived. Else, it is never going to attend to the root of its problems, and is going to continue to require quick-fix strategy work to give it the illusion of survival.

All that is around us is through the conceptualization of individuals. This includes both good and bad things. If a process has been poorly planned or a strategy ill-conceived, it too is because of shortcomings in individual perception and ability. Amongst some of our weaknesses lies one of never seeing the whole picture. We tend to view phenomena form our isolated view point, and we tend to rigorously back up what we believe in, even if it has less than a true standing. Amongst the many things that individualization would be involved in, would be the enlarging of one's own perceptive abilities, so that individuals may see a phenomena for what it is, and so that they may be objective about the observed phenomena rather than attaching a judgment to thereby further skew their already incomplete perception. The scope and possible methodologies that can be applied through individualization are numerous. It is a whole science in itself, which will demand attention if for no other reason than it will provide companies with a definite competitive edge.

Certainly, one can envision entire companies that specialize in the individualization process, just as there are entire companies that specialize in reengineering, and entire companies that specialize in strategy. In terms of implementation, strategy will be the short-term focus, reengineering the medium-term, and individualization the long-term focus. A company may offer all three in a three to five year project, say, or just strategy in a three to five month project, but the company wanting to provide real-value, must of necessity master and provide individualization, which alone can deal with the true root causes of problems and provide lasting value and the ability to deal with any kind of environment.

But why are such trends taking place? Evolution is not a random process. For if it were so, all life would be in the midst of an incomprehensible chaos. However, there is no chaos, and therefore there must be some Principle that is secretly, and even overtly guiding the steps that humankind takes. In that all progress we have made has emanated from the individual, it is fair to assume that all progress we are to make will emanate from the individual too. So far the progress we have made has been through the Einsteins and the Gandhis and the Bonapartes of the world: a few individuals whose power has carried millions of others. Individualization will now put in the reach of all individuals what earlier was the province of a select few - the application of a concentrated inner look to examine the strengths and weaknesses that exist, and the knowledge to amplify and move the strengths into action. In that the key to all previous breakthroughs, and the key to future breakthroughs lies in the individual, Nature has assumed a trend in which the culminating motion is a settling on the individual.

The value of this movement of Nature can be further revealed through understanding what an organization is. Apart from being a vehicle for realizing a mental concept at the level of Matter, an organization is a structure of growth which by virtue of occupying a pivotal role in human society is an important means through which humanity can evolve. Viewed from the bottom-up, organizations consist of individuals. Further, organizations provide a certain reality in which these individuals grow and experience certain forces of and in the world. Through its infrastructure an organization determines the extent and quality of interactions one individual has with another, and the extent and quality of interactions an individual has with vaster external forces. An organization to a large extent becomes a laboratory or play-ground or mini-universe where each individual is confronted with his fears and anxieties and happinesses and aspirations and made to overcome and realize them. Viewed from the top-down, organizations have an influence on the locality or society in which they exist. Once they have achieved a certain critical mass, the organization through sheer economic and political and social power can alter or at least influence the workings of its containing locality and society. Further, through their impact on individuals, who are also the components of society, they have another means by which they can intimately influence the workings and growth of society.

Thus, an organization can have an important impact on how the individual and society evolves. In that current attention is more outward-focused and attention at the level of the individual has been sparse and ill-thought out, the impact at the level of the individual has often been of a negative nature, and consequently an organization's positive impact on society has rarely ever been felt. But if the current inward-moving trend is to be fulfilled, then the sheer position of an organization, coupled with the fact that the organization's primary focus will be the growth and welfare of the individual, will of necessity create a cumulative internal and therefore external environment which will be radically different from the one today.

These two influences will commingle to create an environment which all Nature has been agelessly yearning for. Finally the very act of work and the very circumstance of mundane life itself will be the field by which a rapid and constant human progression will be made possible. We may hypothesize that at least one thing, as has emerged in other inward-moving universal trends, should emerge through this inward-moving trend - the sense of interconnectedness and oneness of all human beings. We will have attained to that peak which today we are in the process of scaling. Only tomorrow will tell what the view from there is like, and what future journeys we may then embark on.

CHAPTER 3

RETHINKING BUSINESS BASICS

Most businesses believe they exist to make money. This is the first in a series of ignorances commonly exhibited by companies. While making money may be a result of the business, and is essential to the continued functioning of the business, it is not its purpose. An intake of oxygen, while essential for our living, is not the purpose of our lives. The purpose is to make this environment, the people within it, the interactions that occur, more aware of and in tune with their splendor and to manifest progressively more of that splendor.

But what does it mean to become aware of one's splendor, and to manifest progressively more of that splendor? It is the contention of this author that life is propelled by a number of laws. These laws are hereafter referred to as 'Law'. If there were no Law, then all life would be in the midst of an incomprehensible chaos. Clearly, this is not the case. There must be, therefore, some Law that covertly and even overtly guides our steps. If indeed there is a Law, then it must exist to achieve a purpose. That purpose is at least to express qualities, forces, and states of existence that lie latent where the purpose itself was formulated. These latent qualities, forces, and states are referred to as splendor. The splendor may take the form of knowledge, power, beauty, or harmony. The splendor will allow humankind to become aware of its innate oneness and interconnectedness with all forms of life, and with the entire Earth and universe and will

result in beings, organizations, and countries, approaching
and treating one another in a harmonious manner.

A business that succeeds in approaching this purpose
will have aligned itself with the implicit Law in creation,
and is sure to become an instrument by which that Law can
be more intricately and completely worked out. While it is
not the purpose of this chapter to discuss the qualities of the
Law, an assumption that such a Law exists, is fundamental
to the arguments that follow. Further, an assumption is
made that human beings are subject to the Law, and so
therefore are businesses, which of course comprise of
human beings. The laws are many, and each has its means,
utility, and purpose in this creation. However, to align with
the one Law is what will increase a business's chance at
'success' as gauged by systems of financial measurement.
A law may be opposed to the Law, and in that respect will
never really generate any momentum of a lasting nature.
Yet it will seem to last, and will attract a sufficient number
of instruments to do its perverse work. A business would
want to align itself with the Law if for no other reason, than
in so doing, the business will have to revamp it's way of
functioning, and in that effort is more likely to conduct
business in a more thorough and enlightened manner, thus
bolstering its own chances of success.

A company which has helped to develop the possibilities
in man will have a higher chance at success. The computer industry, for example, has heightened the human being's
mental possibilities and helped form a clearer and more
complete picture of many aspects of life around. It has
helped the human being define and expand its individuality

and its collective interaction and expression. The physical product and its utility though, is just one aspect. As importantly, how does a company treat its employees and the people it deals with? Does it do what it can to develop the potential inherent within each individual? Is it making of the individual a more knowledgeable, loving, harmonious, and organized individual? How is it developing the collectivity? Is it teaching the individual to look beyond surfaces to tap into the vastness of her being? Is it teaching the individual to work in a dedicated and surrendered manner as though the individual were working to enhance the work of the Law? What net positivity in terms of the direction and intention of evolution is the company imparting or expressing in its day-to-day functioning?

It is the intention and the state of consciousness behind the act that is of importance. The act in itself is not the sole important thing. Whether one is peeling a potato, programming a computer, or lecturing a group on the myriad methods of marketing is not the entire issue. The thoughts, feelings and intention that comprise the act is of importance. For ultimately the most basic acts and gestures are the ones that must express the splendor, and it is at this level that the transformation from doing an act for its end-result, or doing it out of habit, to doing it out of love, must take place. When one addresses a colleague is it with fear and a sense of separateness, or is it with the knowledge and the feeling that in one's depths all are connected and are one? For if all are one in the depths, then in addressing a colleague one is really addressing some part of the self. And if it is oneself that one addresses then surely the whole manner and approach will be different than if in one's mind it is another that one addresses. Similarly, when a company interacts with the rest of the world, is it solely for its own gain, is it in an adversarial manner, or is it to express some of the Beauty that is to be manifested, and is it to create a more harmonious relationship with its larger self? These attitudes will determine how the company performs, and really, whether it will succeed or fail.

Today's emphasis on customer satisfaction is part of that same expression. So is the success and move toward employee empowerment. The movements that are gaining in popularity today are but surface movements and expressions aimed at drawing out the true nature of the Law and creating in the mundane the reality of the Infinite. Industries that are declining are those that are destructive to the expression of Power, Knowledge, Beauty and Harmony. Industries that are failing are doing so because they are failing to align themselves continually with the Law inherent in existence. What they achieved and did yesterday is not what they must achieve and do today. The Law creates forms but then just as quickly uses those forms to create something more complex. If that complexity of expression is opposed or not allowed to develop then the instrument which may have once been an effective instrument but now is not functioning as one, must be replaced by another. Industries that are aligned with some law, but not quite the Law, may succeed for some time, but they cannot succeed for long because the law they are aligned with cannot succeed for long. Any industry's success and failure can be understood when a study is done of how well it has aligned with the Law in existence.   If one is planning to create a business one should think deeply on what it is one is planning to create, and why one is planning to create it. Is it something which is going to express some of the splendor or is it something that is going to oppose the Law? But again, one's ability to understand and see is linked to one's purity either as an individual or as a company, and to develop that one must begin to take a sincere look within.

A second ignorance is to act as though only the short-term mattered. Businesses have a tendency to evaluate themselves primarily by short-term results, and consequently to plan primarily for the short-term. Where this attitude is prevalent, there there cannot be a regard for the long-term and for the intent of evolution which is necessarily long-term. Where this attitude is prevalent, there the planning in all probability is catered toward maximizing short-term profits, and there the programs that invest in the future by taking away resources from the present tend to be frowned upon, and approved only if their utility has been proven. But the realm of evolution does not easily lend itself to proofs, and therefore there is a strong tendency to disregard such programs at the outset. Such an attitude can only be detrimental to the overall health and long-term success of the company.

The underlying intention of existence, where the Power, Knowledge, Beauty, and Harmony are to be expressed at the level of Matter, and where the Infinite is to become apparent in this finiteness, requires a long-term perspective, and a detailed, drawn-out, continuous and consistent effort. Businesses must plan in such a manner that their immediate

and continued actions and plans express more and more of
the splendor over time. If their planning continues to be
catered toward the short-term, they will be successful only
as far as their actions and plans and their results coincide
with what is to be. But that kind of blindness cannot continue to cause success indefinitely. The pressures on and
the mind-set of decision-makers are such that actions must
have an immediate benefit. If the action does not satisfy or
show results immediately it cannot be a worthwhile action.
This mentality has become ingrained in many quarters of
business. The question is what is being done to change it in
the long-term? So long as it is not changed businesses will
tend to place their planning and emphasis on areas which
are not beneficial to their long-term growth and success.
Inertia is a stubborn law to uproot, and it is only by a continuous and consistent effort that it shall dissolve.

An example of the focus on the short-term is a company
which in an effort to increase its short-term profits manu-
factures products without regard to the repercussions their
manufacturing processes have on the environment, and consequently on generations to come. While they are presum-
ably increasing their short-term monetary wealth, they are
simultaneously reducing the health and long-term wealth of
the entire planet. If enough companies do this a threshold
may be crossed that will make any kind of preventative program inadequate. In time the very resources that the company uses in manufacturing will have been depleted and at
the very least, the company shall be unable to produce the
product.

An third ignorance is the scope that businesses may

define for themselves. Oftentimes businesses will over simplify the extent of their influence by believing that they exist solely for themselves. The limits of their decision-making and scope of influence ends where their physical influence ends. Yet, businesses are intricately connected to the world around them. There are their suppliers and customers, the environment in which they are located, their competitors, and their government. They are an integral part of a much larger system, and if they followed a simple rule whereby they treated all that they interact with as part of themselves, and sought the best for all involved parties, then they would benefit the most. Companies acting in isolation, that is, making decisions that affect others, without the others being involved in the decision-making process, and without acting to seek success for the others, can only accidentally happen upon a solution that is in their own best interest.

Consider a company that decides that it must cut its own costs in order to remain competitive. They have decided therefore to exert pressure on their suppliers so that they can reduce their own costs by paying suppliers less. This decision has been made in isolation, without fully understanding the repercussions on suppliers. Supplier A is now unable to supply the part and goes out of business, and the company itself now runs into delays in supplying its customers with products because it does not have enough of the part provided by supplier A. Even though their financial statements indicated that they had had a more profitable quarter, ultimately they are the ones who have suffered. Similarly, on the customer end of the situation, if a business wanted the highest short-term profits, it could sell a faulty product for the full price, and then later refuse to service it. It has succeeded in drawing in the additional cash it was looking for. But when it comes time for that same customer to buy another product that the business offers, chances are that she is going to go somewhere else, and consequently the business has lost out on a potential series of sales. What's more, through word of mouth she has probably informed everyone she knows about the company, and consequently the business has lost so much more in potential sales. Understanding that it is a part of an intricately complex system is key in making good business decisions, and in bolstering a business's chances for success.

Companies that redefine their limits to include the vaster world around them become that much more aware of the issues of different groups, and that much more effective in designing solutions that will satisfy a larger number of groups, thereby enhancing their own chances for success. The nature of a relationship based on harmony is such that one becomes privy to more sensitive issues and more real concerns, which provides some of the detail needed to stay ahead in the world of business.

A fourth ignorance is the tendency of businesses to function primarily on the surface. Just as we live primarily on the surface and are unaware of the deeper parts of our being, so too businesses are unaware of the deeper intentions behind their business. An understanding of these deeper laws will help businesses function more appropriately. Oftentimes, a business does what it believes it has to do in order to become successful. Yet nothing happens. Other times, in spite of what a business does, it is still successful. An example is the case of a company in the rapidly growing cellular telephone industry. Key individuals had no inkling as to who their customers were. Yet they were experiencing 50% annual growth rates. When prodded to understand the customer base, the regional marketing manager replied that the industry was so strong that regardless of what they did, they would continue to grow.

Oftentimes we get stuck in trying to understand business phenomenon by an examination of the most surface-oriented variables, such as market share. We tend to operate in a symptomatic manner, instead of operating by a true understanding of the underlying laws which are making everything happen. We may have attached significant importance to market share, and as a result may get concerned when it drops. Instead of understanding why it has dropped it is very easy to increase advertising to try and get it back up. Our actions have been conditioned by surface movements and in our concentration on making the surface variables look good we have lost sight of the real reasons as to why the surface variables are changing.

If we want to increase our market share in a certain product area, surface laws would indicate that we could reduce price, since there is an immediate correlation between price and buying action. The lower price will stir more people to buy the product. But then, a competitor could lower price too, and the market share that had been gained will revert back to the competitors. Alternatively, the advertising effort could be stepped up, in the hope that the potential market will become more aware of the product thereby stimulating them to buy it, to consequently increase market share. But that misses the whole point. Depending on what your product is, this may or may not work. If your product is something that is aligned with the covert intention, then the advertising will increase the awareness in the market about something which aims at manifesting the splendor more fully, and that may very well work. It is not the advertising that has increased the market share. That was the catalyst. The real mechanism to increasing market share is to understand what needs to be manifested next, in order to increase the amount of splendor. What is it that is needed that will help humanity and help individuals realize the power, beauty, knowledge, love they are capable of? What is it that is needed to help humanity and the individual to see clearly and to realize the depths of their being and their oneness with all around them, and the true purpose of existence? Align with these underlying paths and market share is sure to increase. Align with these underlying paths and more people will be satisfied than currently are.

A fifth ignorance is to believe that we are the becoming we see. It is easy for a business to come to believe that it is the sum of its actions. Everything that a business does defines the business. Yet everything it does issues forth from some source. Every action and idea and plan has come from a silence and a depth. The more a business can consciously link with the depth, the more aware it becomes of its source, and of the source of all its ideas and actions. What it expresses externally no doubt defines it, and is what defines success for the business. But at the same time, of equal importance, is the relationship it has with its silence.

How do the ideas and actions come to the surface? Is it in a conscious fashion, or is it as a momentary impulse? If it is the latter, then there is no reliability to the flow of ideas and the source of inspiration may not always be appropriately tapped.

Yet the very success of the business is dependent on the continued outflow of the correct actions and plans. If the creation of actions and plans can be a conscious process the business has a more defined method to success. Brainstorming has been touted as being the method for generating ideas. Yet on close examination it will be observed that from the conglomeration of ideas, it is in silence that the one idea is chosen, and the right choice is made. A corporate silence of this nature is necessary. An awareness of what lies behind the constant activity, and an active and conscious effort to link with this source of the continued creativity and expressive output is necessary. Businesses may fall into the trap of coming to believe that they are the output, and therefore continue to create in an uncontrolled manner. This could cause a cancerous situation resulting in the premature demise of the business. Introspection and the periods of silence are necessary if growth is to proceed in a wholesome and coordinated manner.

A sixth ignorance is a lack of coordination around a central theme. There are many parts to a business. There are many wills operating simultaneously. The question is whether these wills are aligned with or in opposition to one another. What are the goals of the individual departments? Are the departments playing off one another synergystically, or are they depleting one another? Are marketing, finance, operations, in unison or in opposition? Oftentimes departments are operating according to their own wills and according to an agenda which they have selected as being best for themselves.

There are too many companies where instead of grappling with the real issues departments blame one another, then rest content, assured that through the blaming they have done their useful work for the day, and thereby avoid taking any constructive action at all. They are steeped in a mist of self-righteousness and separated from each other by barriers of contentment constructed by the irrelevant accusations they continually hurl at one another. It is these very barriers that must be destroyed and replaced by a sense of a common work to be done. The mists must be dissolved so that each can see and understand the other and understand how the other is also a part of the self. Where the departments act to complement one another, and act so as to achieve the same goals in alignment with the will of the company, there synergy can take place, and the business as a whole can produce a sum greater than its parts.

A combination of all these shortcomings, the seventh ignorance, creates a business that stumbles and guesses its way through a tremendous maze. It is a wonder that the business remains afloat for long at all. Yet this is what is happening all over the world. By seizing on some element of Truth companies happen to survive from day to day. Some go bankrupt and wonder why. Some are seizing more and more elements of Truth, through the mechanisms of employee empowerment, systems thinking, reengineering, customer satisfaction, strategy planning, executive retreats, consultative selling, organizational flattening, and are beginning to benefit by them.

A company that can explicitly address these ignorances in a systematic manner will be that much more equipped for success, and that much more equipped to become a conscious instrument for the workings of the Law. Even if they have no interest in becoming an instrument of the Law or even if they cannot understand the Law, they will continue to be successful or will increase their chances of success because they are in harmony with the deeper laws of being.

CHAPTER 4

PREDICTING SUCCESSFUL MANAGEMENT PRACTICE

This chapter will suggest a method by which successful management practice can be predicted. In so doing, unsuccessful practices can be avoided to thereby save time and money. The chapter starts out by establishing parallels between modern management practice and quantum physics. It then describes parallels between quantum physics and a realized human's experience of self. It finally describes parallels between modern management practice and a realized human's experience of self. The chapter ties these three seemingly distinct phenomena into one cycle. It depicts why the findings of quantum physics and the realized human's experience of self are good predictors of successful management practice.

Relation of modern management practice to quantum physics

How does modern management practice relate to quantum physics? Recall that quantum physics is the modern day outlook on fundamental particle theory, and has replaced the atomic view held by physicists for centuries. In the atomic view atoms were the fundamental building blocks of the universe. They were solid, indestructible objects and interacted with each other according to fixed laws imposed on them from above. Further, some Force created these particles, the laws between them, and set them into motion like a big machine. All consequent movement is therefore deterministic so that anything can be predicted if everything else is known. Contrast this with the quantum view which finds that the deeper one penetrates into matter the more elusive the fundamental particle becomes. In fact, it is found that there is no fundamental particle, but only a pattern of energy some of which may manifest as a particle. Further, these manifested particles display wave-particle behavior, with the wave signifying the probability with which a particle may be found in some location at some time. That is, the particle could instantaneously appear anywhere across some space-time continuum. Essentially, there is an intricate web of connections that intimately connects all 'matter' at the level of matter.

In many respects the shift between traditional and modern management practice mirrors the shift between the perceived behavior of fundamental particles between the older atomic view and the more recent quantum view.

Consider, for example, the increasingly popular practice of process reengineering. Process reengineering is the practice of focusing on work flows in an organization rather than focusing on functional departments. Many tasks in organizations cut across functional boundaries. For example, in a customer fulfillment process customers phone in their orders to the sales department, the shipping department sends the orders to them, the accounting department generates an invoice, the finance department records the revenues and costs involved, and the marketing department collects more detailed information about each customer.

Most common managerial processes will usually involve several departments. A typical transaction of this nature may take weeks before reaching completion. By directly connecting 'points' in different departments, the practice of process reengineering reduces the cycle time of each individual transaction and in the bargain increases the satisfaction of the customer who now receives the order earlier. Simultaneously, the same amount of cash is generated in a shorter time thus enhancing the company's overall cash flow. Company records are updated in real-time thus providing a more accurate snapshot of the operations, the shipping department reduces its storage expenses because of a reduction in inventory, and the marketing department creates a more accurate profile of its customers. Thus each part of the company involved in the process has benefited.

The older atomic view suggests an isolationist reality which shows up in organizations as myriad departments absolutely and neatly separated from one another. Process reengineering is the practice which is now connecting the departments more intricately and completely to form a 'quantum-view' of the organization. Much like the quantum physicists 'web of connections', modern day organizations are being connected so that the isolationist reality of departments is being replaced by the more effective reengineered organization.

This same 'web of connections' aspect of matter is also showing up as the very successful 'networked organization' concept. Networked organizations is the practice of building organizations such that small sub-organizations within the group can operate autonomously. Through maintaining their small size they are able to maneuver more effectively. Through sharing expenses, research, marketing resources, etc., with many other sub-organizations within the network they are able to behave with the muscle of a larger organization. This is allowing seemingly small and independent organizations to instantaneously act as a much larger organization. It also allows the seemingly small and isolated organization to act instantaneously at a vast distance from its physical location by virtue of the connections through other small units of the network.

Quality circles, too, are a movement away from the isolationist focus propagated by the atomic view. Quality circles is the practice of having a group of employees jointly evaluate products, services, and/or processes. Rather than an issue being examined solely from one point of view, an issue can now be examined from several points of view to form a more informed knowledge 'pattern', in the same manner as particles interact with one another to form the fundamental energy pattern. The practice of bringing together several viewpoints to thereby transcend the narrowness of a few viewpoints, and thereby arrive at a more complete and harmonious endpoint is what has given the quality circle its popularity and effectiveness.

Peer reviews and upward reviews move away from the hierarchical framework where examiner is always the boss, toward a level framework where one is examined from multiple points, in the same manner as the individual threads of a web converge onto its center or focal point. This allows employees to become aware of how it is to work with and for them, so that they may alter their behavior to become more effective in both relationships.

The hierarchical view of the atomic world in which fixed laws were imposed upon the fundamental atoms, has been replaced by the single level of the quantum world, where particles seem to function with an intelligence inherent in them. This shift has manifested as flattening of organizations. Organizational flattening is the practice of reducing the number of levels of management in an organization. Thus, many organizations have reduced the number of management layers from 15 to 3. Of course, with each additional level of management the inefficiency in an organization increases. Decisions take longer to make. Direction decided at the top takes more time to filter down into the ranks of the organization. Further more, the direction and strategy gets diluted or mixed with each levels own perception on the way down. Thus, fewer management layers allows the organization to function more effectively.

The intelligence embedded in the fundamental entity, further, shows up as the principle of employee empowerment, and is a moving away from the principle as proposed by the atomic view, of intelligence being imposed from above. Employee empowerment is the practice of pushing authority down into the organization so that employees themselves can make the day-to-day decisions that need to be made. Rather than referring each decision or thought upward, the belief is that through empowering, decisions can be made at lower levels and therefore more in real-time, causing the whole organization to run more effectively. Further, the practice of empowering employees develops in them an autonomy and sense of responsibility and pushes them toward a more rapid and fulfilled growth.

The quantum view of all fundamental wave-particles being intricately connected, as opposed to the atomic view of independent, indestructible elements, manifests in the practice of systems thinking, and customer satisfaction. Systems thinking is the process of linking a business to its external determinants. Rather than a business operating in an isolated fashion, there are a number of entities to which it is linked and which intricately determine its own success. Systems thinking has allowed businesses to step into their larger reality and determine more accurately how each of their actions will affect them. Customer satisfaction has also grown in importance. With an increase in competition the only way a company can hope to stay ahead is by fully understanding the needs of its customers. But that is not sufficient. A company has to really care for its customers to the point of satisfying them completely. If customers do not like the goods and services provided by the company, then the company is not going to generate the profits and revenues it needs to keep in business. Customer satisfaction has thus become an imperative for business continuance.

The point is that these management practices are the state of the art not because atomic view has been proven inadequate, but because they allow organizations to function far more effectively. Just as the quantum view helps explain physical and scientific phenomena far more accurately than has the atomic view, so also modern management practices allows the organization to function far more effectively than older management practices. Each of these management practices has evolved from a practice, which astoundingly, but not surprisingly, parallels a view of fundamental particles as espoused by the classical physicists. Thus the departmental view, multiple layers of management, order from above, 'tell' principle, and isolationist tendencies, are all behaviors displayed by atoms in the classical physicists view.

Relation of quantum physics to realized human's experience of self

Pushing the analogy further, we will find that the view of the universe and the fundamental particles that comprise it as postulated by quantum physicists is remarkably similar to experiences of the self and world of the realized human being. One way to examine this is by comparing the difference between atomic physics and quantum physics to the difference between the experience of a normal individual and a realized human being.

Atoms are indestructible, solid objects. Wave-particles are a pattern of energy of which some energy may manifest as some particle or the other. The average human perceives herself as a defined physical entity. The realized human is the self in all, that contains all, and manifests simultaneously as the defined individual form that the average human knows her as.

Atoms are indestructible, solid objects. In the quantum physicists world, atoms actually consist of vast regions of space. Within this space are swiftly orbiting electrons, protons, neutrons, which form 'layers' from the nucleus to the outer shells. Similarly, the average human considers herself as a single 'layered' physical being. The realized human experiences herself as a multi-layered entity, with several concentric bodies. Thus, there is a 'causal' body, a 'physical' body, and a 'subtle' body.

Atoms are isolated entities. Quantum physicists propound that the fundamental entity is a wave-particle which is intricately connected with all other wave-particles. The average human on the street believes that each individual is separate and isolated. The realized human perceives that all individuals are intricately connected and in fact are part of the self.

Atoms act as though there is a law imposed upon them from outside. Quantum wave-particles have an inherent intelligence which determine their functioning. Similarly, the average human acts according to societal laws, and that is the reality she faces. The laws are imposed from without. The realized human experiences the seat of intelligence and knowledge as being within herself, and as being the source of all her actions and laws.

Atoms move through absolute space and absolute time, and any changes that occur are due to the movement of independently flowing time. Quantum particles, traveling close to the speed of light, conform to Einstein's general theory of relativity. Time is not an absolute entity, but forms part of a space-time continuum, and in fact time will flow at different rates in different parts of the universe. Space and time are both elements of a language an observer uses in describing the observed phenomena. Similarly, the average human experiences events as occurring at different points of time, within a certain space. The realized human experiences events as present in their entirety in the consciousness of the self. Further, they unfold themselves in this particular space-time environment as events through time.

Atoms, the forces between them, and the laws they follow are completely separate from an observer. Quantum particles have no meaning as isolated entities but can only be understood as interconnections between the preparation of an experiment and the subsequent measurement. Similarly, the average human views everything around her as separate from herself. The realized human experiences everything 'around' her as part of the self, of which she also is a part.

The mass of an atom is associated with indestructible material substance. Quantum particles have a mass which is a form of energy. Similarly, the average human is a solid physical being, with matter as her base. The realized human experiences herself as a consciousness which manifests in part, as matter.

The force between atoms is an entity that is rigidly connected with atoms they act upon. The force between quantum particles is pictured as the exchange of particles. In fact, force and matter are unified, with both having their common origin in the dynamic energy patterns we have called 'wave-particle'. Similarly, the average human experiences forces as being something linked to her interaction with others. The realized human sees matter, force, energy, as all having their common origin in consciousness, and in fact being different aspects of the consciousness. A force can exist independently of any object, and can have its own purpose and existence.

In the classical physicists view all forces need a medium to travel through. In the quantum physicists view forces are entities themselves and do not need a medium to travel through. The average human experiences force as conveyed through voice, action, or movement. The realized human experiences force as a form of consciousness which can exist for its own, separate purpose.

While there are immense parallels between quantum physics and the self as experienced by the realized human, quantum physics is a fledgling science, not even one century old, while 'self' experience has been affirmed and reaffirmed through the centuries. Further, everything found in quantum physics has already been found by the realized human. Quantum physics is today grappling with combining relativity theory and quantum theory to understand the nature of the nucleus, which lies at the heart of every atom. The experience of the self of realized humans however, has generated volumes of insights that have been untouched and unthought of by the average human. Even physicists could begin to take their cues form the experience of realized human beings.

Further, as mentioned earlier, when physicists begin to penetrate the depths of matter it is found that what seemed solid is in fact energy. Thus, the very concept of 'matter' being the base and starting point of human development has come undone. In fact, that belief is flipped on its head and energy itself is seen to be the starting point from which matter manifests.

Could it be possible that energy too is only a form of something else? Consciousness perhaps? If we assume that to be the case then the link between science and experience of the self is complete. The realized human's experience therefore should be the starting point from which we examine and build all other endeavors.

Relation between realized human's experience of self and management practice

While traditional management practice is similar to the average human's view of reality, state of the art management practices, of the kind discussed in the first part of the chapter, can be seen as an attempt to emulate reality as experienced by the realized human.

Let us first consider process reengineering. It is the practice of redesigning work flows along 'natural' paths within an organization, rather than letting them flow in their convoluted manner up and down each department before going on to the next department. Through connecting points in what is normally viewed as isolated departments, myriad connections are being made that facilitate the ease with which different parts can communicate thereby making it more like 'one' whole, rather than like the several distinct parts it has been identified as.

Quality circles is the attempt at having a larger, more informed intelligence and knowledge, an approximation toward the 'seat of intelligence' of the realized human, examine the relevant issue. The traditional practice of having a manager review a subordinates work leaves too many holes in the end-product.

Peer reviews and upward reviews remove the hierarchical constraints of the possibility of learning only from 'above' by allowing feedback from all directions. It is an attempt to treat more equally and with importance that which was traditionally 'below', and of learning from it.

Networked organizations is the practice of allowing global organizations to act locally. The organization has the advantages of rapid maneuverability through virtue of being small, and simultaneously has the tremendous resources to back it up, in terms of R&D, marketing, finance, etc., through virtue of being big. This structure approaches the realized human's experience of self, where the self is one with the all, while simultaneously being the local frame we may perceive her as.

Systems thinking is the practice of linking a business with determinants which had not normally been considered as part of the business, but now are seen to have an important impact on the success of the business. This practice approaches the realized human's experience of self, where the self is not just the individual physical frame, but is just a part of all the rest that is around it. By artificially cutting off the boundaries where the physical frame ends, expected results no longer occur. Only when the self is seen as all, can the unexpected begin to be explained.

Organizational flattening is the practice of removing layers of management between the top and the bottom of the organization. This approaches the realized human's experience of self, where the self is not far-removed from the all, but is in fact one with it. The bottom comes as close to the top as is possible.

Employee empowerment is the practice of empowering an employee to make decisions and take action without unneeded managerial consent within her realm of work. This practice approaches the realized human's experience of self where the seat of intelligence and action resides within the self who is therefore absolutely capable of deciding what needs to be done.

Customer satisfaction is the practice of fully understanding and fulfilling the needs of customers. This approaches the realized human's experience of knowing whatever needs to be known through a direct identification. The need of a customer is not something to be guessed about from a distance, but to know directly as one would know any part of the self. The customer's needs therefore, are fulfilled in the same manner as one would fulfill one's own needs.

Conclusion

The various organizations and business practices we design, and the very quality of our lives will be determined by what we perceive our lives and selves to be. The average human's perception, much like the classical physicists perception, has led to a model of behavior and reality which is proving to be inadequate in dealing with the realities of our world. More often than not specialists, consultants, and visionaries, the 'quantum physicists' or 'realized humans' of the age, redesign the current system based on a more accurate perception of how things are. Many of these redesigned systems have proven to work.

It is the management practices that have not worked which are of relevance. How do we ferret out the effective from the ineffective? How do we avoid spending vast amounts of time and money on something which is destined for failure? An experience of the reality of quantum physicists, and more so of realized humans, will form a sound basis for prediction. As illustrated in this chapter, the management practices which have met with success have remarkable parallels to quantum physics and to a realized human's experience of reality. By experiencing this same reality, knowing what it is that forms the fabric of life, and rending the veils that lock us into our present narrowness and utter insufficiency, we can begin to know which management practices will work and which will not.

We can either construct nuclear reactors and particle accelerators in our houses and study particle behavior under gigantic electron microscopes and elaborate bubble chambers, or we can simply begin to move away from the noise of our thoughts, emotions, and habits, and become the ungarbed entity within.

CHAPTER 5

CHANGE MANAGEMENT

Change Management has become a critical part of many organizational work efforts. While state of the art change management excellently diagnoses the organizational problems that exist, subsequent methodologies for remedying underlying problems are feeble. These methodologies assume that humans are reactionary beings and consequently aim at shortening the reactionary-cycle. As changes occur more rapidly, however, as is the case in today's complex global environment, the only way for a company to successfully deal with change is to effectively remove the reactionary-cycle.

An alternative methodology which aims at removing the reactionary-cycle altogether, by pushing employees into a deeper experience of self is presented here. A panel study, conducted by Auro-Surya, confirmed that through the use of the alternative methodologies suggested here employees become less reactionary in nature, thereby approaching the ideal of bypassing the reactionary-cycle. This enables companies to react more easily in real-time to the complex global environment.

This chapter discusses the necessity for change management. Further, it discusses the limitations of state of the art change management. It suggests a more effective approach to change management, and finally presents details of such an approach.

The necessity for change management

Ideas and practices in management have seen a rapid evolution in the last few decades. This is not surprising given the rapid evolution of the world. Problems have refocused from the large to the small, from the macro to the micro, from the global to the individual. Thus, while in the early to fairly recent twentieth century world attention focused more on achieving harmony between nations, and on fundamental race issues, today the focus of attention is more on problems of an individual nature. It is not a question of fighting for one's country any more, but a question of dealing with drug abuse, difficult personal relationships, starvation, or simply, personal anxiety, frustration, and depression.

That is not to say that the problems have become trivial or inconsequential. It is just that the future development of the world necessitates a focus and a resolution of these personal issues and matters before a more puissant synthesis between the large and the small can take place. These critical problems necessitate our delving into the very nature of existence, into the very nature of ourselves, and into the very nature of our interactions in groups.

Ideas and practices in management have shown a similar pattern. In the initial stages of business competition it was more important to understand such issues as what the company was going to produce, how it was going to produce it, which other companies were producing similar products, and how one company was doing in relation to another. This emphasis on the macro-management and strategic direction of a company, and its relative place within a given market, gave birth to such practices as strategic planning, marketing management, financial analysis, cost accounting, and economic analysis. With the advent of global competition and the increasingly complex and varied environment, these practices have been further researched and perfected. They stand today as necessary methodologies that a company has to employ to even think of competing in the global environment.

Just as problems in general have moved from the realm of the macro to the realm of the micro, so to ideas and practices in management have had to move from the level of macro-planning and assessment to a level of micro-planning and implementation. The broad lines having been laid out, and the direction of a company having been determined and planned, it becomes necessary to understand and execute the details. Just as a painter first outlines a painting, and then fills in the details and various colors, and just as a sculptor sculpts the general shape to then chip in the details and intricacies, so to managers have to move from the realm of a strategic plan, to the realm of fully understanding how it will be worked out in its detail.

It has in fact been the experience of many companies that their plans even after implementation have only rarely yielded the productivity and efficiency improvements they had envisioned. In implementing details for any macro-level plan a company is inevitably thrust into the realm of people. For it is people who conduct the day-to-day work. It is people who are the accountant and the marketer, the engineer and the scientist, the researcher and the scholar, the analyst and the salesperson. And even though a company can plan out what these people should be doing differently or should learn anew in order for the broader plan to work, it is rare when the plan is actually realized.

We are thrust into a whole new level of complexity. The macro-level plan assumes that if people are told to change their behavior or their work habits it is done. The macro-level plan assumes that introducing complex computer systems to shorten internal cycle-times will work, because people will simply discard their age-old habits of working on paper in favor of working on a computer. The macro-level plan assumes that a change in the fundamental way of thinking and perceiving the marketplace can occur overnight. This however, as thousands of companies all over the world will attest to, is not the case. People are complex entities. They must be understood. This is what change management attempts to do. Change management attempts to factor in the human variable in any broad and high-level plan. Change management requires understanding who these people are, what motivates them, and how they currently do their work. It requires understanding what is involved in their current job, what changes are being asked of them, and how they will react to the changes being asked of them. Further, it requires understanding how best to change the way they do something now to how they should be doing it in the future for the plan to work, amongst other issues.

Limitations of state of the art change management

State of the art change management follows a superficial approach in that it assumes that there is a fixed pattern of emotions that each person will display when asked to change. Further, it assumes that the employees will eventually change when the new job is thrust upon them. Modern day change management will analyze an employees current way of doing the job. It will, based on the strategic plan, design a new job description that the person must now follow. It will include sessions to explain to a person that change is inevitable and necessary to deal with the new realities of the world. It will include sessions to even explain that loss of an old way of doing something to a new way being thrust on them is like the death of a loved one. Of necessity the employee will experience a period of denial-rejection-anger-acceptance, which in the absence of any change management techniques would take a much longer time to go through than in the active presence of them.

Change management thus tracks the surface of experience and attempts to condense the reactionary cycle so that the new behaviors demanded of the employee will occur sooner rather than later. It does not however get to the root of the problem. Nor does it aim to remove the reactionary cycle altogether.

Change management techniques involve designing surveys to question the employees about many aspects of their job and work environment. The surveys are designed to understand the degree of resistance that employees will show when the change does occur. They seek to understand the culture of the company, how consistent the culture is with the planned strategy, and how strong the current culture is. They seek to understand how much stress the employees are currently experiencing in the absence of the planned change, how successful past changes have been in the company, and how important the employee perceives the change to be. They seek to understand how strong the support for the change is throughout the organization, and how effective the middle-level managers, whose skill-set will play a major role in determining the success of the change effort, actually is. They also seek to understand how ready the organization is for change, and how able the organization is to change.

While this analysis is an excellent starting-point and begins to pinpoint where the focus of the subsequent efforts need to be, it is the subsequent efforts that are lacking in substance. Much like the efforts of a doctor in fully understanding the symptoms of the problem, the change analysis thus far has succeeded in understanding the symptoms of the organizational problems. Unlike a doctor's approach however, where a wealth of methodologies on how to treat the underlying problems exists, change management has feeble and unsatisfactory methods of actually dealing with discovered problems. Most likely, it has not even understood the underlying problems, but seeks solely to alleviate the manifesting symptoms. The current repertoire of change management methodologies may include pep-talks, change seminars urging people to change, discussions on the inevitability of the reactionary cycle, and venting sessions.

These methods derive their validity and strength from surface rather than deeper dynamics. They are thus insufficient
in dealing with the crux of the problem.

No where in the entire process has there been any study
on or any action related to the crux of the problem. The
issue of what a human is, of what habits are, has been
unknowingly unconsidered, or only accidentally and only
briefly touched upon. It is the hope of the practitioners of
change management that the techniques they have used will
result in the necessary changes. Given the lack of attention
on the real underlying issues though, any success can only
be serendipitous. The problem is not in getting a person to
change from one description of a job to another. Nor is the
problem in condensing the supposedly necessary cycle of
reaction. The problem is in understanding the nature of
habit, and in realizing what must be done to break old habits
in a more effective and accelerated manner.

Day after day a person performs a job in one way.
Further, there is a certain set of beliefs that the person has.
Suddenly some new competitive information arises and the
management of the company decides that the company has
to change its position in the marketplace. This requires
reeducation of many of its employees and a different way of
thinking and operating on a day-to-day level. The current
state of the art of change management is a potpourri process
in which the old job, new job, emotional reactions, and surface analysis, are all thrown into a cauldron. Six to eight
months later, say, it is reexamined to see if the old has successfully changed into the new. The problem is compound-
ed by the fact that by this time the original plan no longer

holds. The environment has changed again, and again a new plan has been created and requires the employees to discard even their new job descriptions and new reeducation in favor of a newer job description and a newer reeducation. Today's competitive, global environment has accelerated the pace of change and its consequent need to adapt to it rapidly.

Designing a more effective change management program

So long as external programs that do not consider the nature of the human being are thrust upon the employees, the desired changes will occur only by accident. First, an enlightened change management process structured around the true nature of an individual has to be designed. Secondly, some means to assure that employees can internalize the change process so that it becomes a living part of them is necessary. Otherwise they will be constantly reacting to changing environments without ever catching up to it, and without ever becoming masters of it.

In its essence a successful change management approach has to urge the employee to begin to look within and understand what he or she is. On a day-to-day basis each seems the sum of his thoughts, emotions, habits, memories, and actions. An individual acts a certain way with one person, and a certain other way with another person. There are always a few stronger thoughts, surrounded and infiltrated by myriad others, and a few key desires which dictate many of the actions of the individual. The individual has a series of habits, and displays emotions when certain external and internal stimuli present themselves. As such, at first glance, it seems the individual is a reactionary being. Naturally then, as is the case today, the emphasis of any change management effort will be on reducing the inevitable reactionary cycle's cycle-time.

So long as the individual remains a reactionary being, then no matter what the change, it will always cause a reaction, more likely negative than positive, invoke the age-old habits, and prevent the individual from changing from his current way of thinking and acting to another way of thinking and acting. So long as individuals continue to perceive that they are a conglomeration of ideas, habits, emotions, desires and actions, they will want rigidly to stick to that, despite any external pressure, for fear of losing their individuality and personality. Their experience of being a reactionary entity is thus further bolstered, and becomes more difficult to alter.

And so long as individuals continue with this view of themselves it will be impossible for corporations to react dynamically to external environments. Further, it will be impossible for corporations to truly capitalize on opportunities as and when they present themselves. Change management will never really succeed in effectively managing human change in an organization. Of necessity, if a corporation wants to be able to implement its plans and wants to become a master of the dynamic external environment, it must create an environment in which the change process is easily internalized at an individual level. This means that individuals have to begin to examine themselves, and begin to experience if in fact they are the conglomeration of ideas, thoughts, feelings, emotions, and habits that they thought they were.

When a change is announced in a company, rather than flow with the emotion of frustration, for example, the employee should begin to observe the frustration. By flowing with frustration the employee becomes completely absorbed in it and believes himself to be that emotion. By observing it he finds that it subsides much faster than if he had become involved in it. Similarly, when a change is announced a series of thoughts may be initiated. For example, 'Oh God, what will happen to me.' 'Will I still have my job 6 months from now.' 'What will happen to my children if I lose my job.' Et cetera. Rather than flow with the thoughts the employee needs to observe them. He will find that they are separate from him, and indeed he is not the thought, but something that stands back silently, calmly, even as the thoughts create their havoc.

Once this ability to stand separately from the emotion, thought, and habit, is attained, then only will the employee be in a position to internalize the change process. For once the employee has stopped being a reactionary being, then a certain mastership over change can begin to manifest. For from the silence of the depths all thoughts and emotions are like superficial waves which cannot effect the essential quality of the being. They come and they go but the true nature remains undisturbed. It is this process which alone can effectively handle change, and it is this process that should become the focus and crux of any change management effort. Rather than continue to attempt to change the surface habits, change management should cut to the core of the issue and begin to deal with the reality of what a person is.

Change management though, and the focus on detail, rather than on the broader, vaster plan is a new emphasis and turn of the attention in the world of management. As more and more companies continue without satisfactory results, the very nature of change management will evolve, of necessity, to deal with the crux of what humans are, and how best to make them ready for change.

Implementation of a successful change management program

A change management program which includes a methodology by which change can be successfully assimilated is presented here. The successful change management program would conclude with the process of assisting employees in assessing the reality of their being reactionary entities. The entire process, thus, would include up-front sessions to convey to employees the importance of change, survey analyses to understand which areas of the organization should receive critical attention, and the reactionary-being assessment, aimed at altering the reality of employees experiencing themselves as reactionary beings. It is this last step which is crucial in assisting employees in internalizing the change process, and in becoming that much more ready to handle change.

A prototype has been implemented by Auro-Surya which aims at making people aware that they are not simply a reactionary being. A primary feature of the prototype allows individuals to track their reactions in an electronic diary. Thus, as and when an employee experiences frustration, anger, or depression, say, they make an entry into the electronic diary stating too, the length of the reaction, and its intensity. The intensity can vary from mild to severe. This very act of becoming more conscious of one's reactions begins to separate one from the reactions. This is an age-old psychological truth and has been documented with some depth in Sri Aurobindo's Synthesis of Yoga.

Auro-Surya conducted an elaborate test, using a panel of 20 people, to confirm this age-old psychological truth. The panel members were given a variation of the diary, and asked to track the type of emotion, its length, and its severity, several times a day. At the end of one month there was a marked difference in the attitudes of self, as experienced by the panel members. Almost unanimously, every member migrated from the experience of being a reactionary being, toward the experience of being an entity separate from their reactions. The findings are illustrated in Figure 1:

As can be seen, there is a marked downward shift in the experiential-curve. Almost every member experienced themselves as being less 'reactionary', and in fact more 'separate from their emotions'. The implications of this finding are phenomenal for any change management program. If such a reaction-recording system were used in any change management effort employees would become far less reactionary, and thus more able to change successfully.

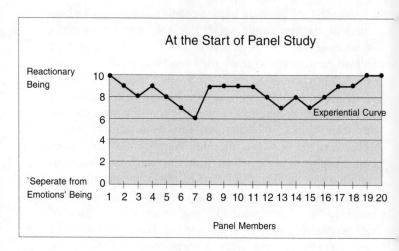

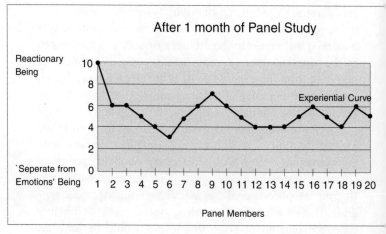

Figure 1. Experiential Curves at Different Times in Panel Study

Rather than react with every change thrust upon them, thereby lengthening the change process, employees would remain more centered in the depths of their being, thus eliminating a lot of unnecessary reactions.

While the panel was restricted to the examination of reactions, the Auro-Surya prototype delves deeper into the human psychology. The model of human psychology used is based on Sri Aurobindo's Integral Yoga, and was chosen after an examination of several models of human psychology. In this view the human being is comprised of several different beings with distinct properties. These are the physical being, the vital being, the mental being, and the subconscient. The various beings combine to form different sub-beings which have qualities determined by the combination of their parent beings. The subconscient surrounds and supports the beings and sub-beings, and acts to perpetuate their separate existence. Further, the range of emotional reactions experienced by human beings arises from the different sub-beings. The prototype has been designed as a semantic net, with each sub-being as a separate node. The properties and possible emotional reactions arising from each sub-being are attached to each of the affiliated nodes.

The primary function of the prototype is to record reactions experienced. The secondary function is to assist and educate users on the origin in the being where the reactions arise from, what the properties of that part of the being are, how the parts of the being are interconnected, and what specifically, can be done to deal with a specific reaction when it arises. Through allowing users to access multiple views of a human being, the prototype further bolsters an individuals experience of being something other than a bundle of reactions. Users can thus search the system to understand why and how the reactions they experience occur. Further, once the entries are made into the diary, the prototype automatically indicates which part of the being the reactions arises from, and suggests specific ways to deal with the reactions.

Thus, for example, if a reaction of fear is experienced, the prototype highlights that fear arises from the 'lower vital', and recommends that deep breathing and visualization of the breath entering the lower vital (region below the abdomen) should be followed to remove the fear. Beyond bolstering the experience of being more than a reactionary being, the system helps the user more fully understand the emotion and even remove it. Current state of the art change management aims at shortening the reactionary cycle. The methodology discussed here aims at resolving the root problem, by removing the reactionary cycle altogether.

Conclusions

Change Management has become a crucial process in the implementation of many organizational work efforts. Whilst state of the art methodology pinpoints what organizational problems need to be addressed, they lack in their strength of actually making change happen. The methodology presented here deals specifically with that missing piece of helping employees successfully assimilate change. This methodology aims at altering employees' experience of being a reactionary entity through pushing them into a deeper experience of self.

Once the reactionary activity as experienced by employees is reduced, they are far more aligned with the change process because they are no longer reacting, and thereby obstructing the change effort, but are accepting, and therefore flowing with the change effort. The implications of this change in employee attitude and ability are truly phenomenal. Organizations will now become more able to react to external changes in real-time, thereby gaining higher mastery over their environments.

CHAPTER 6

MONEY

Money is a valuable force which is indispensable to the development and fullness of existence. In its reality it should be used to enhance the consciousness of individuals and of humanity. Yet, it is being used in a variety of other ways. This chapter will examine some of these uses. Further, it will suggest why it is being used in this manner. Finally, it will suggest alternative uses for it aimed at enhancing individual and collective consciousness so that organizations of tomorrow may more effectively lead the world in a harmonious and many-sided development.

Some uses of money

Some pieces of art sell for thousands and thousands of dollars. A Picasso was recently auctioned for twenty-one million dollars. It is a painting, and can certainly bring out a perspective or an aspect of beauty which provides its viewers with satisfaction and a glimpse, or at best a vision, of deeper aspects of life. Its value is in its potential of awakening the viewers to that deeper perspective that may ordinarily be unconsidered by them. But because people are in possession of money that they do not know how to use, they rush to buy the object which wise observers and art critics have praised as valuable. This in-rush of money causes the price of the desired object to rise deliriously. The value of the money has in the bargain been bastardized. Further, the art object which may have inspired a larger public is now the sole property of an individual. The art object now takes on an entirely different meaning and is equated more with its perceived monetary worth than its ability to inspire and satisfy. Being of such high monetary value it now draws the attention of thieves and scoundrels, thus contributing to criminal intent and activity in society.

Money has lost its meaning. At one time, not too far in the past, fifty thousand dollars/year was considered an excellent salary. Today, graduate students from leading management institutions are barely satisfied with salaries of eighty-five to one hundred thousand dollars/year. The problem is two-fold. First, due to inflation and the continuing rapid decline in the value of money, essential and even non-essential products and services have escalated in price. Thus more money is needed today to buy the same set of items that yesterday could be purchased at a much lower price. Secondly, an unfortunate attitude has infiltrated our minds and habits. This is the attitude of saving money for the sake of saving it. Thus, while it is essential to save money to prepare for one's old age and for emergency circumstances, in many cases saving money has become a hobby and the end rather than the means of our existence. Many want to invest their money where it will offer the highest rate of return. There is no consciousness as to how the institution where the money is being invested at is going to realize that rate of return. They could very well be funding a crime ring in some inner city, or funding an arms company that is providing weapons to extremist groups around the world. There is no sense of responsibility for how one's money is being used. The primary interest of most is in getting the promised rate of return.

The easy access to money, especially in western society, has spawned another unfortunate tendency - that of transience. Myriad consumer products ranging from clothes to electronics to automobiles are discarded prematurely. Instead of caring for an object and taking the extra steps to maintain it and prolong its life, at the first signs of deterioration people will discard the object in favor of a brand new one. This habit has also promoted a false sense of power. People believe that they are powerful because they have the money to acquire what they need, and to quickly replace items when they desire to. It has crystallized an attitude of acting primarily in the short-term, and today people and corporations are suffering for it. The easy access to and frivolous use of money has also promoted the tendency amongst consumers to hoard. Thus, people are in possession of more clothes and shoes, for example, than they actually need. They may end up never actually or rarely ever wearing these items. But it remains in their possession, and remains unutilized. This amounts to waste. Further, many companies advertise to appeal to instincts in human beings. They successfully create an image of a brand which causes people to be willing to pay more for it. In fact, if consumers do not then buy that brand they begin to feel unwell, and plan on how they might acquire that tea or perfume or pen or whatever else it is that has been so cleverly advertised, and which in reality they may not even need.

Whilst large cities tend to be prime business centers

where many want to be located, in today's age of global telecommunications it is possible for many companies to conduct business from anywhere. Yet, because they have the money or can easily raise it, they will spend a fortune to enter an already overcrowded city. The warning signs against entering the city are many. The most obvious is the rapidly escalating real estate prices. By pushing their way into that city they contribute to overburdening its already taxed infrastructure. The population and pollution levels go up. The demand for entertainment and recreation begins to exceed the supply. Traffic congestion increases. Crime levels increase because of the increasing number of wealthy people in the city. The psychological price of living in that city rises. Dissatisfaction levels increase. The entire atmosphere of the city begins to get coated by a layer of frustration and gloom.

Companies too, display the unfortunate tendency of wanting to accumulate money rather than spend it effectively. Money has a value. Money has a force. Its best use is in circulation, not accumulation. It takes on its greatest value when it is spent. Yet the tendency of society is to accumulate it. Consider the recent stock market example in Bombay, India. Companies that went public received an inrush of money as a stamp of the public's approval and belief in the future of those companies. The millions of rupees that many companies received was not used to enhance the production facilities and capacities of the company. Rather, it remained in a state of limbo and most companies used the money to restructure their financial positions. That is, they rearranged their financial assets to unload debt. The money was not used for a productive end. It was used so that the companies looked better on paper. It is a natural law that the more one breathes out the more one can breathe in. If one is in the habit of expelling breath in a shallow manner, then the breath taken in is also shallow. Similarly, when one does not use the money in their possession, no new money will come to them. The most successful businesses are those that are not attached to their money, but are able to spend it freely on new projects and in developing their own capacities and capabilities. Money will go where it is used. And it will go more where it is used most effectively to raise the consciousness of humanity as a whole.

In the field of education, the norms that dictate our society cause many children to pursue an education which will assure them of receiving the right diplomas and certificates so that they can acquire the right job and the right amount of money when they are older. And that very money is then used to make more money, and used to destroy its value, and used seemingly to fulfill the million desires which are impossible to fulfill, and which like a clever virus transmute into another million desires if ever fulfillment seems close, thereby to ensure that the same petty and destructive cycle continues unendingly. What about the value of learning to acquire knowledge? What about the value of learning to understand and know the secrets of Nature? What about learning for the love of learning? What about the value of education in developing traits and abilities and drawing out the inherent uniqueness in each child? What about learning to become the master of one's character, and learning to fulfill a sublime destiny? This vicious circle that most of society is in, falsifies the use of money and causes even children to cast aside these precious opportunities of pursuing their inner dreams, in preference to the pursuit of diplomas and a falsity which will assure the continuance of today's depraved society.

Countries that have money, and even those that do not, have spent it on building weapons of mass destruction so that they may have what their neighbors have, and be equally equipped to play their part in destroying their fellow beings, countries, and our world. Those billions of dollars being spent in the construction of weapons could and should be used as a force to benefit humanity, not as a means to lay waste what has been developed through thousands and thousands of years. In countries with large bureaucracies money has acquired another perverse use. Many public servants require additional incentive in the form of bribes in order to perform their regular jobs. Thus, ministers have been known to take bribes to issue licenses to industrialists; police officers have been known to void traffic tickets if offered a bribe; and even bus drivers have been known to drive at an accelerated pace if incented with additional money. This very money should be used to shrink the bureaucratic organizations, grow the private sector, and retrain the public servants so that they may begin to do something of use.

Why is money used in this way

Why does this distortion exist? Quite simply, its roots are

in the belief that each human is separate from every other human. If I believe I am separate from another then my money must be used for me. And then, what are all the ways in which this 'me' can achieve its satisfaction. How many different kinds of foods and liqueurs can I consume? How many and which models of cars can I buy? How many houses can I acquire for my seasonal use, and how many species of animal can I raise as pets? How many different designer made shirts and dresses can I purchase? How many varieties of jewelry can I collect, and where can I go on vacation this year so that others may realize that I have a lot of money and do not know what to do with it? In what other ways can I flaunt my power? In what ways can I satisfy this 'me', this individuality, this piece of being, which surely and absolutely is separate from the rest, and surely and absolutely deserves special treatment and periods of joy through fulfilling all the million suggestions that constantly arrive in its realm through the course of the day and the night.

And so the ignorant thinking and the ever-wanting cycle continues. People use all their energies in pursuit of things which assure that they will remain unendingly in those same restricted grooves of being. It is these very grooves of being which determine the quality of one's thought. Thus the cycle continues forever. Yet it is this very habit and structure which must be broken with the agent that has realized it in the first place. Rather than perpetuate the smallness which we think we are, money must be used to help us break out of this meaningless cycle which makes us the slaves of our desires and the impoverished warriors and upkeepers of our destitute thought.

The state of our Earth with its race wars, drug wars, rampant crime, impoverished children, starving communities, and trapped human beings is largely the result of the thoughts and desires of those who have the money, but do not know what to do with it. These are the millions who make up the driving class of societies across every country of our Earth. This belief that money must be used for small satisfactions keeps it tied up in a groove which makes it lose its value and pauperize its user. That very money, directed in another way, can loosen the hold that the million varieties of meaningless fulfillment have humanity gripped in, and through the enlightened thought and action that can follow, can reverse the wars, crime, poverty, destitution, and most importantly, the impoverished view, unknowingly, that each has of him or herself.

Alternative uses

Imagine when money is no longer used to acquire land in a place like Tokyo. That same money can then be used to develop another piece of land in some underdeveloped place on Earth. Imagine when money is no longer used for idle and conspicuous consumerism. That same money can then be judiciously spent to meet the necessary outer, and deeper needs of people, thus developing them to become more conscious human beings. Imagine when money is no longer used to build weapons of destruction. That same money can then be used to enhance the understanding and relationship between countries. Imagine when money is no longer used to bribe public servants to do their regular jobs. That very money can then be used to educate these public servants and build a noble, productive, and efficient public sector. Imagine when money is no longer used to acquire drugs which destroy our children and able adults. That same money can then be used to help the children grow so that the special qualities they possess will have a chance to flourish, and that same money can be used to help the adults to better realize their places in the harmony of life.

Money in its true role must be used to raise the consciousness of humanity. Why is this the rightful goal? And what does raising the consciousness of humanity mean?

All our present efforts are aimed at experiencing joy in whatever form we know how to experience it. Thus some may take a walk in the country side, others indulge in drug use, yet others chant hymns of adoration, and others go for a hunt in the forest. While all actions stem from our perception of the world and our perception of what will help us become happy and joyful, not all perceptions, either of the world or of what will bring us joy, are complete and true. While drug-use may provide us with an immediate and temporary euphoria, more often than not it has destructive after and side-effects which harm us both physically and psychologically. In fact the short-term joy is vastly overshadowed by the long-term pain inflicted upon us. Yet, through no fault of ours, we perceive that its use is beneficial, and therefore use it. Our own perceptions are a function of our experience and evolution, and the perceptions we have at the moment are necessary for the experience we need to lead us to our own further growth. Yet, there is a subtle balance and always a choice that exists in our every thought and action. We can continue to follow the actions which are in harmony with our limited perception or we can choose to enlarge ourselves so that that limited perception begins to yield to a more enlightened perception.

The seed contains in it the mighty tree, and even the minute trickles on mountain tops enlarge in their downward flow until they empty out into the vastness of the ocean. These metaphors of existence embody the concept of growth. We too are here to grow into mighty trees reaching toward the sun, and into vast oceans reflecting the whole atmosphere in our silent depths. Growth is the inevitable law of life. Everything around us is in a phase of growth. To assist in that growth is to enter into harmony with the hidden laws of life, and to fulfill overtly the covert intention of all individual and world movements. The very act of consciously assisting in our growths will provide us with the unending joy that we unconsciously seek for through the myriad groping of our thought and action, many of an ignorant and self-defeating nature, throughout the course of our everyday existence.

Money used to assist in this inner growth, would be money used for the rightful purpose. Our growth could take many forms. We could develop our physical natures to become strong, flexible, supple, and beautiful, and to possess stamina, endurance, agility, and speed. We could develop our artistic qualities and appreciation for beauty, our writing abilities, our speaking abilities. We could develop our thinking and reasoning abilities, and even our capacities for intuition, revelation, and inspiration. We could develop qualities such as sincerity, humility, gratitude, perseverance, aspiration, receptivity, progress, courage, goodness, generosity, equality, and peace.

There is no end to the ways in which we can grow. Yet, current norms and ways of being tend to arrest our growth and slow it down, and this is what must be changed through the judicious use of money. Put to its right use money will assist in the transformation of Earth to make it truly a golden globe moving happily amongst the stars.

CHAPTER 7

EDUCATION

Education is a powerful enabler for global change. The success of our future institutions and Earth will depend on the ability of the children of today and tomorrow in leading it wisely. This chapter provides a perspective on the long-term help that businesses can provide in the field of education. In trying to elaborate the perspective the goals of the education must first be made apparent The higher and wider the goal, the more complete and potentially effective will be the help that businesses provide. The goal should be such that the current problems faced by the world are not only solved, but a future harmonious and fulfilled development becomes possible. Thus, there are two components to the goal. First, to ensure that the current problems are solved. Second, to ensure that children are allowed to develop in an integral fashion such that will best bring out the uniqueness and special traits they have to offer to the world, thereby allowing it to develop in a more harmonious and fulfilled manner.

The goals of education

In fulfilling the first goal, the thinking and habits that have led to the creation of today's world must be replaced by a more enlightened thinking and action that allows the world to develop in a different manner. Therefore, children should not be taught in the same manner that education had proceeded yesterday. A discussion of the nature of this education will follow shortly. In fulfilling the second goal, the resistance from adults, who may claim that their perception and thinking are the culmination of human ability must be overcome. Such an attitude can only stifle any creativity and inherent uniqueness that children may have to offer.

Today's inequities and problems are a result of the narrowness in thinking which has plagued us as a human race thus far. The structures that we build around us and the reality that we have created are the result of our perceptions of ourselves and our world. And this perception is the result, in large part, of our thinking abilities. The more enlightened, harmonious, and enlarged is our view of ourselves, the more enlightened, harmonious, and enlarged will be our thinking, action, and the resultant reality in the outside world. For starters, we must reexperience ourselves along a truer tract. We have come to believe that we are the mind and the body, and that our potentialities stop with the abilities and capacities we have exhibited so far. Thus, we may believe that we are only capable of such present and confirmed mental phenomena as reasoning, recalling, imagining, and calculating. We may also believe that there are only a limited number of physical abilities, such as strength, speed, flexibility, etc., that we are capable of. These self-constructed barriers, built by letting our limited perception dictate the possibilities of reality, act to deter any further expansion in our abilities and capacities.

Any education must first, therefore, aim at letting an as true a figure and reality of ourselves emerge, as is possible.

Any education must aim at transcending the beliefs we have of ourselves as human beings. But this will only happen if we allow that which is true and enlightened within us to emerge; and if we have the patience, endurance, and commitment to keep the old ways of thinking and being, as nothing more than an indication of what we have been on the way to what we are to become.

To experience this other way of being, all that we have been thus far, and all that we allow to fill our active consciousness, must fall silent. The old cup of tea must be emptied before the new tea can be poured into it. In the silence of the mind and the heart, that which is luminous within us will be allowed to emerge. So long as the continued disturbances of our everyday thoughts, emotions, and ways of being continues we shall be unable to contact this luminosity. The education of tomorrow must allow for the luminosity in each child to come forward. Adults have been conditioned already, and for them to even perceive of the luminosity is far more difficult, if not from their point of view, a chimera and an impossibility. The adults must be educated to allow the development of the children to occur in a manner which will be completely different from their own development.

If children are educated in the same way, with the same perceptions of themselves and the world as their parents, the distortion of yesterday will be perpetuated unendingly. The personal, social, economic, political, and environmental inequities will continue until some cataclysmic event, brought about by the sheer ignorances of today's living shall force the current structure and modes of being to collapse under the weight of the accumulated stupidity. Then humankind might understand that its beliefs are inadequate, and begin seeking for this other way, which can be sought for at this very moment, before any of the catastrophe actually occurs. The current path is one of destruction and of wasted effort. It would be far more fruitful if we consciously allow the luminosity to come forward, through the children of today and tomorrow. Rather than the mind, or the emotions, being masters of our lives, the luminosity must be made the master of our lives, with the mind, emotions, and body relegated to their true position as its instruments to do its enlightened work.

While education must emphasize the coming forward of the luminosity, it should simultaneously emphasize the right development of the mind, emotions, and body, so that these instruments may be made ready to assist in the work of the luminosity.

Thus, the mind as an instrument must allow clarity in thought. It must have a good memory, reasoning ability, and a quality of inspiration and articulateness. But its shortcomings must be realized too. The mind is an instrument which dissects all problems. The nature of the mind as we experience it is such that it cannot conceive of a problem in its entirety. Its dissecting behavior therefore creates complete truths of only partial truths, and is primarily responsible for the narrowness we experience in ourselves and in the world.

This narrowness of thought is exemplified in any domain of life. Thus, in religion for example, even though each religion has gifted man with a distinct and unique vision of the Truth, individual followers always believe theirs to be the best, highest, and only complete truth. Examined for the Truth in them, and what they stand for however, it will be found that "Paganism increased in man the light of beauty, the largeness and height of his life, his aim at a many-sided perfection. Christianity gave him some vision of divine love and charity. Buddhism has shown him a noble way to be gentler, wiser, and purer. Judaism and Islam, how to be religiously faithful in action and zealously devoted to God. Hinduism has opened to him largest and profoundest spiritual possibilities." Yet the followers of each of these religions believe that theirs alone is the only truth and the only reality, even when it is clear that each religion has brought forth a different aspect of the one Truth. "A great thing would be done if all these God-visions could embrace and cast themselves into each other." But the narrowness of thought and the incapacity of the mind will not allow it.

Similarly, in the realm of business, the mind would have us believe that the sole purpose and meaning of business is to generate money. Yet, as more and more companies are experiencing today, they have to be concerned with a whole host of other issues, such as the people who work for them, the environment they work in, the products they manufacture, amongst other concerns, or they will tend rapidly towards extinction.

The mind is incapable of seeing all sides of a problem simultaneously. Teamwork has arisen as a remedy for this shortcoming, by attempting to bring different views together to more holistically address problems. Even though people come together with diverse viewpoints, and even though they share them, yet more often than not a deadlock situation results. One person, even after hearing another person's views, and possibly feeling how true it is for them, refuses to accept it, staying inalterably within their own view. Each one is still stuck within their own model. The models do not synergistically meld to yield the whole truth of the situation. And this inability is at the crux of many problems that we experience in the world today. It is only when all the knowledge from all the viewpoints shall be fairly and accurately known in one 'mind', that the inability shall be transcended. But it cannot be known by mind as it exists today. Another faculty, the luminosity, which thus far has existed in the recesses of the being, governing life through the myriad obscurities and internal veils, must step forward and become the master of the being. Then, and then only, will humankind move forward progressively and harmoniously, successfully altering all the worlds problems.

It is only when the luminosity steps forward that a problem and its solution will be known in its entirety. For the nature of the luminosity is such that it becomes one with the object of attention, while simultaneously transcending it. It knows, therefore, all there is to know about the object. Further, the mind is locked into a relative arrangement of time and space. This causes the human to experience and know life in only one possible way. Yet, as Einstein had begun to uncover, Time and Space are not absolute, but relative. In some sense one has to step outside of them to properly grasp them. The luminosity would, at will, transcend this arrangement of time and space and allow the human to experience and act on situations in a completely different and possibly far more effective manner.

The emotional education must proceed to make each being a master of his character. Children must cultivate calmness, and yet be able to do with power and enthusiasm the task to be done. "It is a misconception that we are born with a certain character which it is impossible to change. The process of change must begin by a sincere discernment of one's own character." "Children must be taught to observe, to note their reactions and their causes, to become the discerning witness of all their desires, and all the movements of their natures. They will find that they possess two opposite tendencies in the character. Along with the possibility of the expressing ideal, will also be concrete elements which represent the battle they must wage to make the realization of the ideal possible." Thus, through overcoming the fear that constantly arises within themselves, they can eventually become courageous.

A vast majority have allotted the pursuit of happiness as a goal of life. This is a deformation of a profound truth. The nature of existence is delight, but the goal of life is to express more concretely and completely the inherent luminosity. The belief that the goal of life is to be happy, coupled with the belief that the character is fixed, has provided justification to the unregenerate parts of the being to continue living as they have. It has also provided an unfortunate mechanism by which an enlightened movement immediately meets with resistance and downright disbelief. Thus, saviors have been nailed to the cross, 'witches' have been burnt, physicists and forerunners of tomorrow's humanity been ridiculed, jailed, or condemned. The domination of the emotional part of the being has become masterful, and makes it all the more necessary that an enlightened education aimed at overcoming the barriers to experiencing luminosity be immediately developed and executed. Once the emotional part of the being has been educated, its vitality and power will quicken the process of bringing the luminosity forward, and further, will provide ongoing assistance in the right government and action of the luminosity.

The education of the body must proceed by first recognizing that it is a being of habit. The correct habits to ensure a healthy and long life should therefore, be inculcated in the child from birth. The body must become strong, flexible, supple, and beautiful. The body must be developed to possess stamina, endurance, agility, and speed. But again, just as in the development of the mind, there is no reason why the development of the body should stop here. The body must be made plastic, to the extent that its very structure can be altered at will. It must become light so that all inertia is removed and it is able to move in a free and unrestricted manner. Once the laws that govern our mind and being are transcended, there is no reason why the body will have to retain its current shape and functioning, which are the outcome of the relationship it has developed with its environment. A new relationship will develop, and therefore too, a new form. The qualities of plasticity, lightness, etc., will enable the new form to be a far more effective instrument for the transforming intentions of the inherent luminosity.

The assistance that businesses can provide

How best can businesses help to fulfill the afore-mentioned goals? Businesses by their very nature, are well poised to battle the inequities that face humankind. Viewed from the bottom-up, businesses consist of individuals. Further, businesses provide a certain reality in which these individuals grow and experience certain forces of and in the world. Through its infrastructure a business determines the extent and quality of interactions one individual has with another, and the extent and quality of interactions an individual has with vaster external forces. A business to a large extent becomes a laboratory or play-ground or mini-universe where each individual can be molded through the interactions they have with one another, with the organization itself, and with vaster external forces. Through being restructured in an enlightened manner, so as to make people more flexible in their attitudes and ways of being, businesses can function to reduce the resistance people will have to new modes of functioning and being. Viewed from the top-down, businesses have an influence on the locality or society in which they exist. Once they have achieved a certain critical mass, the business through sheer economic and political and social power can alter or at least influence the workings of its containing locality and society. Further, through their impact on individuals, who are also the components of society, they have another means by which they can intimately influence the workings and growth of society.

Thus, a business can have an important impact on how the individual and society evolves. Further, businesses hold a vital place because they are the agents through which a vast amount of money power flows. And money power is what can be used to invest in educational systems that will ultimately let the world flourish and reach a level of unending stability and harmony.

Specifically though, businesses can help in several ways. Businesses can have in-house education for their employees. This aspect cannot be overemphasized. Regardless of what the future holds, the current reality is the starting point, and can either assist in the future development or fight it with its own inflexible structures and modes of being. Parents and adults of today have to be educated so that they become aware that their own perceptions and modes of being are limited, and that they should not hold as the ultimate standard what they believe in.

Businesses could also directly support children in their education through building special schools or donating money to programs which will assist in tomorrow's development. If businesses are to pool together to start schools, they must do so to create ones that are at the forefront of educational thought. To create a school that perpetuates yesterday's perceptions would defeat the purpose of the help that can be given. The help must be enlightened. Schools that are created should have the following guiding principles in mind.

"One, nothing can ever be taught. The teacher's business is to guide, to suggest, to answer questions, to stimulate reflection and curiosity - but never to impose." It is only when an inner curiosity develops that the children themselves will learn what is being presented to them. To dump on them theories and facts and figures is a sure way of deadening their natural curiosity, and at most will only develop their capacity to remember.

"Two, children must be consulted in their own growth." It is this principle that will ensure that tomorrow's world will not be a replica of today's. Children have within themselves a uniqueness which must be developed and brought out so that it can effectively change society and the world. To impose a fixed system of education is counter-developmental. To tell children that they have to study a certain thing in a certain way amounts to blanketing any creative urges. While children must have a fundamental knowledge of the world, its mathematics, science, language, etc., in order to relate to everything else and in order to provide a basis from which to act, at the same time the emphasis must be on developing their individuality and their uniqueness.

A stable system lies in diversity. Diverse elements provide the basis for a complex unity. If all children were taught the same thing and made to function in the same way, then society would degenerate from a lack of vitality. The children are the architects of tomorrow's world, and the secret blueprints stamped in their hearts must be allowed to be realized. Diversity alone, will assure the harmonious development of the world. We can look at various systems in our world for examples of that. Complex eco-systems assure life. Imagine if all the various insects and animals and plant-life were replaced by one species. Immediately, tremendous disorder would result because of the lack of diversity. The entire species would turn on one another for food and if they did not destroy themselves in that manner, the ensuing lack of originality which would cause everything to be examined from one point of view would certainly result in its demise.

Empires that have flourished in the past have been those comprising of diverse cultures. The moment the Roman Empire tried to impose one culture on its constituents, the empire spelt its own death. Similarly, the Indian Empire flourished when it comprised of a variety of cultures acting in harmony. Even the breakup of the recent communist block iterates this same phenomenon. Where diversity is suppressed there the life-streams are turned off resulting in the degradation and eventual demise of the whole system. From a philosophical point of view too, the world would not have diverse cultures, plants, species, if it were not in its best long-term interest. No two leaves are alike, nor are any two fingerprints. Diversity is the fundamental building block of any harmonious system, and an educational system that supports diversity, through letting children develop in their own unique ways, will assist in propelling the world toward a glorious future.

Education by projects will allow this uniqueness to develop. Children will choose a project that interests them. Something in the project chosen will spark off another interest which will determine the choice of the next project, and so on. Thus one child's path will end up being completely different from another's, thereby allowing their inherent uniqueness to develop. Of course, the projects must be designed to include language, mathematics, science, history, etc., to allow the harmonious development of the thinking abilities.

"Third, we must work from near to far." Children should learn about their immediate environments before learning about a remote continent. They should learn about the problems and needs of the people of their own vicinities and countries, before learning of remote cultures.

A program of this nature must necessarily be aimed at the long-term if it wants to have a significant and beneficial impact. This does not preclude companies from acting in the short-term, however. Children today face critical day-to-day problems. Drug-taking, gang-joining, child abuse, school dropping out, sexual activity, are amongst some common ones. Businesses can begin to battle these problems through awareness building. Businesses can invest in and create groups that fight these problems at the roots. Businesses can create enlightened television programs and fight to remove the perverted ones.

But let us not forget, even while we come up with a hundred different ways to treat the symptoms, that it is not the child who is responsible for the problems it is facing. It is the adults, it is we, through our intolerances, and warped preferences, and maligned creative forces, who have created the reality that children face, and it is only through a long-term program that the very ignorances that shape our thought and action can be changed, to thereby make the world a better place.

Sections in quotes are words of Sri Aurobindo and The Mother, of Sri Aurobindo Ashram, Pondicherry, India.

CHAPTER 8

TOWARDS COMPREHENSIVE BUSINESS EFFICIENCY

Generation of profit is the anchoring principle in the running of corporations today. It is in fact more than the anchoring principle - it is the purpose of Corporation today. What is Profit? Simply, it is the difference between the revenues a corporation generates and its costs.

A study of Nature will reveal that each of her structures has been created so as to minimize the expenditure of energy. At a micro-level atoms are packed together in the closest possible manner. At the macro-level objects and forces will follow the path of least resistance. In our day-to-day existence we may notice that birds that fly a lot and fish that swim a lot tend to be streamlined thereby minimizing the expenditure of energy in moving through their respective mediums. Seeds in fruit, similarly, are also streamlined so that when splattered onto the ground they may more easily penetrate into Earth. Nature is the ultimate designer and one of her design rules seems to be to get more from less.

In that regard corporations attempt to mimic her and run as efficiently as possible, by maximizing the difference between revenues and cost. After all, corporations too are a construct of Nature. Nature, however, has had thousands of years to perfect the plant and animal kingdoms. Corporations are a fairly recent construct and it is not surprising, therefore, that they have vast room for improvement in becoming energy-efficient like Nature's other manifestations. The generation of profit has served as the formula for achieving this efficiency. Unfortunately, in defining efficiency, rather than considering the comprehensive scenario, inclusive of both the short-term and the long-term, and inclusive of all necessary components of the internal and external systems, modern businesses primarily concentrate on the short-term and on only some aspects of their internal systems. Further, they simplify the reality of each of the internal system components, including human beings, by equating them to machinery.

Thus, whilst corporations intentions have been to run efficiently just as Nature runs efficiently, corporations have instead approached the definition of 'efficiency' from a "vital" standpoint rather than a comprehensive and more realistic "mental" standpoint. What does it mean, though, to be centered in a vital standpoint? The vital principle is that which seeks to achieve, aggrandize, conquer, glorify, bring to fruition. It stands as one of the predominant influences in the shaping of humanity. Consider human-beings as consisting of a physical principle, which urges the development of the body and physical force; of a vital principle which animates them, gives them their drive to live, to satisfy desire, to grow, and to conquer; a mental principle which is embodied as the mind and is responsible for sensing, feeling, morality, aesthetics, intelligence; and a psychic principle which drives toward joy, love, and a final reality of abiding by and bringing to the surface this deepest and superior driving principle.

Beings concerned primarily with meeting their physical requirements, of building their bodies, of increasing their physical force, of getting a shelter over their heads, of getting their daily food, of meeting just their fundamental urges, but who have no other pursuits may be considered to be physically-centered. In man's past, civilizations have existed which sought only to fulfill themselves physically. Beings concerned primarily with fulfilling vital requirements, of satisfying desires, growing by conquest, greatening themselves at the expense of others, may be considered to be vitally-centered. This seems to be the dominant active principle of contemporary humanity. Within a mentally-centered principle there are several possibilities as the range is wider and more complex. At one end mentally-centered living may involve the pursuit of intuition and light, holism, and that which integrates to create a synthetic combination of possibilities, and at the other end it could mean living a Philistine existence dictated by sense and feeling, in the pursuit of what has been supposed as being good. Different forms of mentally-centered living are becoming more alive now. A psychically-centered existence could tend to a feeling and knowledge of brotherhood with all and a spontaneous love and joy regardless of circumstance. Few have attained to this level.

Any individual has all four of these principles existent within him in various degrees of combination. A predominantly physically-centered individual may be driven to meet just the basic needs of his body with little or no concern for the vital, mental, or psychic principles or what they represent. This dominance of one principle over the others could occur in any combination and will determine the outlook and nature of the life led by a person. Corporations, comprised of individuals, tend to become what is projected out by the dominant or group of dominant individuals in the corporation. In fact, just as a human-being has a body, a life, a mind, a psyche, so too does the corporation have a body, a life, a mind, and a psyche. The body of the corporation is made up of numerous people, who are its numerous cells. The life of a corporation is comprised of the various flows of money and of information which make possible its internal activity and connect it to the vaster world around it. The mind of a corporation is comprised of its guiding principles - its mission, vision, strategic objectives, and plans to achieve them, and its culture - the set of unwritten rules that guides employee and employer behavior. A corporation is as much a living entity as a person is, and just as a person has that deep psychic-principle which is the hidden master and guide, and which chooses experiences so that the being may grow in accordance with its destiny, so too does a corporation have that deeper psychic-principle which will arrange the experiences it needs to grow in accordance with its destiny.

By definition psychically-centered corporations would have a central body in which everyone in the corporation, themselves psychically-centered, projected out one principle of brotherhood, joy, love, and deep and overarching wisdom. It can confidently be stated that no such corporations exist today, because not even a handful of people the world over have attained to this principle of operation. There are mentally-driven individuals who are the idealists, dreamers, and thinkers of humanity. But as is true of most individuals, so is true of most corporations, that they are predominantly vitally-centered or at best Philistine in their approach thus trying to do what is considered right without really appreciating what is being done.

Most individuals are constantly in the pursuit of means by which their thousand desires can be fulfilled. Most individuals are seeking always to obtain more personal wealth, to gain more power over others, to satisfy their continual hungers, and to make an end of fulfilling the never fulfilled, ever-emerging desires. These are the individuals, the mass of humanity, who drive and comprise the majority of her corporations, and it is their world-views or lack thereof of one, and their petty desires, and common-place thought, that generates the agendas of the dominant vitally-centered corporation. Naturally then, profit as defined in the vitally-centered approach, and which equates to power and most likely to additional funds in the shareholders pockets becomes the driving force behind the functioning of corporations.

Consider the frenzy of activity at the corporate level all over the world today. Companies are being acquired with a vengeance, thus fulfilling the vitalistic urge to grow and to dominate. There has been a rationalization that this will make them run more efficiently - but even that has not been proven to date. Companies are being down-sized in order to increase short-term profits, boost short-term stock prices, thus enriching shareholders, again fulfilling the vitally-centered need to grow rich at any expense. People working for these corporations are not viewed as being people, but become machines - utilizable, billable, expendable, replaceable. And so long as there is a price and a cost attached to a person, and no consideration for the vast complexity potential within each, it makes complete sense, from the vitalistic viewpoint, to dispense with them when it seems that profits may be compromised.

This attitude of treating people as though they were machines cannot endure. People have minds, and a psychic, and when treated like machines a mass of dissatisfaction and a flow of negative attitudes and dysfunctional behaviors begins to manifest and eat away and change any positive atmosphere in the corporation. Soon the entire workplace is completely devoid of the respect and love of fraternity, with only a sense of fear, anxiety, anger, and depression in its place. This mass and flow pervades the workplace, seeping even into the machinery, production facilities, laboratories, and computing environments, imbibing more and more of the corporation with a sense of negativity, short-sightedness, and desperation. Yet treating people in this manner has yielded the profits the vitally-centered corporation has so desired, and even though the body, the life, and the mind of the corporation are being continually subjected to cancerous influences what does it matter so long as the desire for immediate wealth has been fulfilled?

While Nature requires efficiency in her systems, as is evidenced by all she has created, corporations as they exist now have attained to only a first and underdeveloped form of efficiency. For unlike Nature's Efficiency which is comprehensive and all-inclusive, with each component prepared with full consideration of every other component, and each component contributing towards an ever-superior and harmonized whole, corporations' efficiency is vitally-centered and has to go through iterations of improvement before it can seemlessly dovetail into and contribute to Nature's harmonic whole. For the reality is that even though corporations may be maximizing the difference between revenues and monetary costs, they have not even begun or barely only begun to realize and account for the costs to Nature, costs to society, and costs to humanity that they continually create by virtue of their myopic operational reality.

Each time a corporation extracts raw materials from Nature, or pollutes the environment with by-products that emanate into the atmosphere or flow into neighboring bodies of water it is increasing the costs to Nature. Firstly, Nature has a finite supply of raw materials, and secondly a beauty which once defaced takes years to redevelop. Corporations need to become aware of these realities and factor these costs into their daily activities. Each time a corporation downsizes, or even if it simply operates at its preferred mode of being, the anxiety-ridden environment it has fostered guarantees a sustained outflow of disgruntled and disillusioned employees and ex-employees. These people continue their lives in society, and may spread the illness of their work environments into their homes, communities, and cities thereby pulling down to some extent the whole of society. These costs need to be factored in to the costs of running corporations. Each time a corporation produces a product that reinforces humanity's urge and natural tendency to remain vitally-centered it is doing humanity a disservice. For the aim of Nature is to evolve humankind to a level of higher complexity and capability, not to hold it in some unfortunate groove of being forever repeating vitalistic behaviors. The costs of producing product and service without regard to what is best for humanity's development is a cost to humanity and needs to be factored in to the costs of running a corporation.

Man has not included all the variables in his equation in the computation of efficiency, and therefore corporations function at a sub-optimal level. The equation defining maximum efficiency must itself be changed to include corporations' real impact on Nature, society, and humanity - not just what Wall Street analysts have so myopically, and in typical vitally-centered fashion, presented as being the final indicators of efficiency. There must clearly, in the long-term interest of individuals, society, Nature, and corporations themselves, be a shift in their operating principles so that higher levels of mind-centered operations becomes the driving force.

Vitally-centered behavior is so deeply ingrained in society that all of society will have to change in order for mentally-centered principles to truly become operative. Politicians, bureaucrats, customers, employees, will all have to realize the inadequacy of the present principle of operation in order to begin to be open to another mode of operation. Yet for all society to simultaneously change does not seem feasible. It seems that again, if we turn to Nature, the path by which this change can occur becomes more apparent. Nature progresses by steps. Thus, animals did not suddenly appear all over plant-dominant Earth. An isolated one-cell animal, with a more intricate internal system, and a means for locomotion appeared first. Then more and more one-cell animals appeared, to be followed, gradually, by more intricate and complex forms of animal life.

Similarly, we can expect that at first there will be one or two corporations operating from whatever mental-level they can. In fact, one can already see several mentally-centered endeavors beginning to emerge and take root within the vitally-centered corporation. Thus, movements such as flattening of hierarchies, streamlining of operations, systems thinking connecting the corporation to a larger external reality, have begun to manifest and take root. As their success becomes apparent, more and more movements, and more and more purely mentally-centered corporations will emerge. This will lead to the manifestation of more complex mentally-centered corporations and the continued and irresistible pursuit of the upward curve, until even the psychically-centered corporation finally shall manifest.

Naturally, as with the evolution of all subsequent forms on Earth, animals were able to do all that plants could do and more. Thus whilst plants are alive, can assimilate nutrients, and multiply, animals can eat, digest, multiply, move, sense, and do more. The later forms are always more complex, more capable, and more adaptable than earlier forms. Similarly mentally-centered corporations will be more complex, capable of all the results that vitally-centered corporations are capable of, and more. Not only will they yield product or service, but yield too profits, happier employees, use more knowledgeably the raw materials provided by Nature, and align themselves more naturally with the covert intentions of Nature. They shall be a synthesis of a larger set of possibilities and shall push individual and collective functioning to a more complex and capable level.

Being driven from a more comprehensive mental view-point corporations' actions will naturally be more consistent with Nature's intentions. Thus less of the costs assumed by Nature, society, and humanity will result, and the overall efficiency of the corporation as a construct of Nature will increase. Profit will still be the driving force for achieving efficiency, but it will have factored into it the hidden costs to Nature, society, and humanity.

Life beckons always beyond. For corporations to become centers for true complexity in tune with the demands and needs of Nature, and to operate as efficient constructs of Nature is an undeniable step in our continued and inevitable upward ascent.

CHAPTER 9

THE NEW PARADIGM

A hurried mode of operation accompanies the running of companies, organizations, and projects. This malady is superimposed upon a general lack of ability to accurately envision and define the goals of companies, organizations, and projects, and further, to effectively complete the tasks required to fulfill the goals.

Consider, for example, the arena of consulting. Today there are thousands of consulting companies covering every conceivable aspect of management. These companies can be specialists or generalists. Thus, there are strategy specialists, reengineering specialists, change management specialists, human resources specialists, financial management specialists, marketing specialists, accounting specialists, and information technology specialists, alongside a spate of generalists. The first question is why do these consultants exist? Why do thousands of companies require consulting help in so many different areas? Why are thousands of companies around the world relegating their responsibilities to external specialist and generalist groups?

The company has a choice in hiring and can hire the same people who work in consulting companies, hire even the people who train consultants in consulting companies, and set up a consulting department in their own organizations to do the same work that they hire other companies to do, at a fraction of the cost. Yet they do not do that. Why? Is it because they have a pressing sense of urgency, that the solution, or a perspective on the solution has to be gotten now, and it really can't wait until tomorrow? If so, what is this pressure on thousands of companies all over the world that makes them act in this manner?

It seems everything must be done more quickly. Speed dials on telephones, quicker air and surface transportation, express meals, express check-ins, and express check-outs have become the norm. As a human race we seem to be going through some kind of time-contraction. More has to be packed into less. The more we can do the more we have lived. We are being led to the limits of a certain way of being. At its roots this whole movement is one to become more dynamic. However, rather than being a movement from the core of our being, rather than the dynamism having a soothing quality and embedded as it were in a foundation of peace and puissance, the dynamism is of a surface-nature and is characterized more by hurry and waste. While the intent is to create a dynamism based on peace it seems some secondary movement, some offshoot or perverted or diminished motion of the original intention has seized us and has control of our endeavors and is moving feverishly to fulfill its possibilities, which judging by the increasing harriedness and rush in which we find ourselves in many spheres of life, must result in an exhaustion and final bursting of the surface possibilities.

Led by surface movements such as desire to become richer, desire to own more, desire to dominate, the inevitable outcome must be a realization that dynamism based on surface movements is insufficient. If dynamism is to exist it must be based on a deeper principle and status of being.

Or is the movement of abundantly hiring consultants taking place because companies truly are unable to approach their own problems in an objective and complete manner and therefore need an objective and specialist or combination of specialist views to help suggest alternatives to their problems? The inability and incompleteness of isolationist view-points is a proven fact in world history. From the religious battles of old, spurred by the belief that the oppressor religion was the one and only way for all humanity, to the ethnic-cleansing in the modern world as evidenced by the Serb-Moslem struggle in Bosnia and the Hutu-Tutsi struggle in Rwanda, from the debates about the shape of Earth and its relative position in the universe to the modern struggle between abortion alternatives, proponents in separate camps have always felt assured that what they believe in is the only truth. And that inability to accurately see the whole, to accurately consider all aspects of an issue in a harmonic fashion is the very way in which the human-mind operates. It is the characteristic functioning of the mind to break knowledge into components and then seize on and consider only one component of the entirety as the whole issue. Given this mode of operation of the mind it is no wonder that there are so many consultants who have to become specialists in some particular area, in order that the management world may continue to operate without falling apart.

The general condition of harriedness and the general condition of incomplete or narrow visioning are the products of man's own way of being projected out into his management beliefs and style, and naturally forms the way that he manages businesses, organizations, and projects on a day-to-day basis. Management activity proceeds from an urge to be dynamic, powerful, and effective. In reality companies and individuals end up wasting time and money, arriving at sub-standard and non-implementable results, and exhausting the individuals involved in the execution of the project.

Internally managed projects, too, more often than not meet with the same fate. Plans to implement a project are charted out under pressure to finish by some time, regardless of the actual details and realities of the work to be done. "If we had this product in a year we would be in good shape," says some decision-maker. After six months have elapsed and it is found that in reality the project is still two years away from the end on what had been originally planned as a one year project, it is decided to double the number of bodies on the project to finish on time. Millions of dollars more are spent, and at the end of the planned time-line it is decided to scrap the project altogether because it seems impossible to even finish it at quadruple the expense and quadruple the time.

Yet while the project is proceeding it's progress is judged by the number of hours each person has worked on the originally planned tasks. If there were fifty tasks to be completed, each of an estimated fifty hours duration, then regardless of the actual work done, once fifty hours have been clocked against one task that is deemed as finished. In reality only one-fifth of the work to be done may have been completed. Clearly project management is an art, which requires a very precise yet encompassing view. Men are incapable with their current mental-tools to accurately plan a project. Projects are judged in terms of time and money. Usefulness of people is judged in terms of the number of hours they clock in a work day. These metrics reduce human beings to machinery. And machinery was produced to do the same task again and again, as many times as possible, without break-down. By human standards a machine is dynamic, powerful, and effective. And a human who emulates a machine to work as many hours as possible, doing one task after another, is also dynamic, powerful, and effective. The whole activity of the business world seems to stem from this urge for getting a lot of things done fast. This is because human consciousness and activity is focused primarily on the material and vital aspects of being.

Yet existence is multi-folded. The work environment and active dynamic of our life is a mixture of four lower folds of existence. These folds comprise of matter, vitality, mentality, and a psychic or soul-fold. But these folds are not uniformly existent or mixed together in equal proportion to one another. In fact, it seems that the material fold is dominant, with folds of vitality, mentality, and soul having correspondingly less influence in the current organization of our world. Thus, even though at the higher end we are mental beings, we are not the highest mental beings possible, driven exclusively by the dictates of the psychic-being within, but mental beings subservient to the material and vital components of existence, with currently little or no effective or visible interaction from the psychic-fold at all.

In reality our activity, our existence is a flowering out of four higher folds of existence. But the flowering is taking place within the confines of matter and therefore is as yet a distant replica of its original strain. The higher folds of existence are those of Truth or Existence, Consciousness-Force, Bliss, and Supermind. Imagine Truth to be the light of a thousand suns, Consciousness-Force to be the inherent ability of all those suns to conceive and execute instantaneously, Bliss to be the joy of all the rays of those thousand suns pouring out like laughter, and Supermind as being possessed by these three and being the dynamis through which all here in our ever-evolving world is held first in a harmonic, loving, yet all-powerful and all-knowing embrace, before being released into its play of evolution.

Whilst this is the nature of the seed, it has been planted in a soil of matter, which is in itself a diminished, a distorted, and a completely folded-over form of the original Existence. The light of the thousand suns therefore does not shine out, and it appears to us as black, dense, and inert instead. The vitality and dynamism in its form of harriedness and impatience, so important in our lives today, is a diminished, a distorted, an inwardly folded-over and consequently impotent form of Consciousness-Force. The growing psychic being, growing through its struggles and travails in an environment dominated by the inertness of matter, and feeling and experiencing at first only sorrow, pain, and fear, is a diminished form of Bliss. The dissecting, biased mentality readily assuming its narrow vision to be the apparent whole, and assuming its means and methods as paramount in the uncovering of knowledge, is only a first and diminished form of Supermind.

We are a tree in growth and cannot be judged now by the

child-like and at best adolescent twigs which have only just begun to stretch toward the stars. Our activity today is a mixture of a mental-physical and mental-vital type, in which ideas, thoughts, and reasoning are placed at the service of the physical and vital impulses and agendas, to fulfill and serve them. We cherish growth. But the growth proceeds and is a slave of conquest and subjugation. We grow by domination, and it is a key principle responsible for our efforts. The more we can dominate, devour, conquer, the better we are for it. And our mental efforts, our management, our way of running our lives, is aimed at fulfilling this implicit urge of our yet-evolving society.

Thus executives rush around the world, bill their clients, pretend or feel sure they are doing useful and productive work. Managers judge progress not by the actual work done, or idea worked towards, but by the number of hours clocked, by the number of dollars billed, by all the metrics of perceived dynamism, embodied so well by a machine. Public companies rush towards the quarter-close, with a majority of their initiatives being dictated by actions that will help to raise their immediate stock price, and being dictated by being perceived as being busy, fruitful, and productive. Sometimes trying to look busy may actually mean that one is working productively, but more often than not, businesses thrash their arms and shout about aimlessly creating an illusion of being productive. Stock market analysts, removed from the actual scene of work, and themselves subject to the same mode of operation as the harried companies they assess, buy into the aimless illusions being created. General investors and the ignorant public, encouraged by the incomplete and inaccurate renderings of analysts, invest money to keep this harriedness and incompleteness alive. Companies continue to hire the public. Thus a vicious circle in which inefficient and inaccurate modes of operation are encouraged is unendingly perpetuated.

Man himself is not to blame for this rapid plight in which he finds himself though: for man's activity is only the out-flowering of the higher levels within the structure of matter. These principles of Existence, Consciousness-Force, Bliss, and Supermind, cannot manifest here in their glory all of a sudden, but have to assume the nature of the substance in which they have incarnated, become one with it, and slowly, over eons begin to change it so that more of their native characteristics emerge within the evolving matrix. Thus, at some point the narrowness and incompleteness in perception and knowing of mind will merge with the principle of all-comprehending Supermind; the struggle and travail of the psychic will merge with the principle of delightful Bliss; the immature and trickling flow of life or vitality will merge with the principle of all-powerful Consciousness-Force; and cowled-over and deadened matter will merge with the liberty of Existence.

Consciousness-Force began to manifest in the matrix of Matter as the principle of Life. Thus the barren rock and empty seas and surging volcanoes of old admitted the principle of Life, or rather yearned for a more conscious movement and to feel, and the yearning called the Consciousness-Force from its native plane to press down onto the matrix of matter and push out of it the secret Consciousness-Force already there, to produce Life. Then

Life, manifest now as plant and tree, yearned, or the secret principle of Supermind embedded within as a folded-over and disguised Inhabitant yearned to know, and Mind began to manifest within the matrix of Matter and Life. Animals appeared on Earth. But Mind itself wanted more of its complexity to come forth, and as a result the semi-conscious being of man was created.

Man, in the bulk has through the last thousands of years remained a being driven primarily by physical and life-forces. He has been satisfied being who he is, remained what he is - a thinking being, thinking primarily of ways in which to fulfill his life-desires. He has multiplied in abundance and is allowing Nature to establish through this settled solidity, a firm foundation on which a rarer strain of man may be established. Once the form had become stable in its complexity of matter-life-mind, the principles within yearned to know, to love, to be, and today out-breakings of this completer and more complex strain of humanity with a more active form of the higher principles of being are beginning to appear.

Yet all that we have, all that we are today, our cities, our technologies, our urge for conquest, is the result of the mental-vital and mental-physical way of being. Only now are we beginning to bang our heads and bodies against the inner and secret doors. Man's frenzied movement across Earth, his incomplete mental-vital management of projects and mental-physical approach to life, with its resultant wear and tear of the physical, vital, and mental bodies, must begin to make him yearn for another active principle of being in which this wear and tear, anxiety, frustration, depression, anger, and all the other outbreaks of his mode of existence are replaced by a more joyous and fruitful way of being.

Witness the bestseller lists replete with an increasing number of books dealing with the inner and deeper ways of life, the outbreak of yogic and occult-oriented societies and organizations all over the world, the content of movies and television programs turning more towards questions of the why, how, and what of life, and the advent of the globe-encompassing Internet.

And yet it is not man who is yearning, but the Inner Inhabitant, the guest from the higher planes, who is pushing now, who is forcing now another principle of being to come into existence. It is the inevitable result of the growth of the tree. The tentative twigs testing their force of being through preliminary life and mind experiments must now become firm and solid in Consciousness-Force and Supermind, and manifest as foliage-laden branches curving gently over Earth underneath because of the increasing weight of their ever-ripening and pregnant fruit.

The pressure to perform, to out do, to conquer, to devour, to be first, to drive unendingly, must result in dissatisfaction - dissatisfaction in the current ability to achieve, dissatisfaction to really do effectively, dissatisfaction in really managing the project, dissatisfaction to solve the problem, so that a new principle of being is forced by the global, escalating pressure to come finally into effect. The incomplete perceptions, the displays of anger, of sorrow, and the upsurgings of all that is seeking to be replaced may increase for a time; the utter mismanagement, the ever tiring executives, the resource-wasting companies raping Earth to provide oil and fuel and products to its blinded customers and managers, may continue until an unbearable pitch is reached, in which this entire structure, this entire matrix of matter-life-mind has no option but to surrender to the principle of being submerged in its depths.

And then at the birth of this new principle all that has characterized today's hurried, myopic, and narrow management shall be offered up in a gesture of surrender, and the mismanaged planning, budgeting, implementation and way of being will disappear into the past, or will begin stalking silently towards its grave. There will, just as animals chose to remain animals, be those who choose to remain men, and operate as such. But the new principle once operative will reorganize Life in much the same manner as Mind reorganized Life when it first appeared. The magnitude of change will be as radical as when Earth leaped from animal-dominated forest-life to man-dominated city-life. A new principle characterized by the psyche, by the supermind, shall become operative.

Instead of the constant meetings between management, which end where they began, in back-stabbing, politicizing, narrow-view fighting against narrow-view to exercise its dynamic and God-given right, a silent-knowing shall manifest. And then what is right and true shall happen. Earth will not be plundered for its oil to fuel jetliners which carry the harried executives in search of vaster territories to plunder and more money to waste. Those decisions will be made which raise the consciousness of humanity, and they shall be made and implemented through specialized consciousness's who interact with one another harmoniously and as if

One. The left-hand will not slap the right-hand so that its own narrow motives may be fulfilled, but act in unison with the right so that their combined strengths, perceptions, and force of being can join to create a more organic and embodying solution. Money will flow to where it can be of service for the greater of two works; not as now, where it flows because of an attitude of devouring, or because of the manipulations of back-stabbing politicizing. The project manager will enter into a silence, concentrate on the task at hand, and offer it to the Guide within, who will instruct what the plan will be, what resources will be needed, how long it will take, and who precisely can help in its development.

Whilst all this is in the future, what must be done now, in the interim? The evolutionary path is inevitable. Matter shall become Existence in its full liberty, Life shall become the power of Consciousness-Force, the Psyche shall possess the bliss of Ananda, and mind shall possess the light of the all-comprehending Supermind. The means of getting there however, are up to us. We can either continue on this maddening path until the mental-vital-physical structure of our existence collapses with utter incapacity, or we can consciously assist in nursing the aspiration for light and turning towards the principle within to usher in its reign.

Our entire existence, life and its activity, organizations, business, and management, is the play and working out of forces which in their final analyses are working to crystallize and make a reality the inevitable evolutionary goal of Nature. Regardless of how we act now the end will Be because it is the goal. In that regard, destiny is fixed and is unwinding now through all the upheavals of our modern age. Yet within the broad journeying of Earth's destiny, we are within limits free-players and can assist in ushering in the inevitable.

Why should we do this? Why should we worry about doing something which is inevitable? Because if we do we can avoid a lot of unnecessary destruction. We can avoid the senseless destruction of our natural resources and the destruction of peoples and cities. We can avoid the history of some nations, who inadvertently slipped into slumber, only to be awoken by the rudening onslaught of invaders. We can begin to cut down on the waste of time and money, of mismanaged projects, companies, organizations, and countries, and lead our world in a more conscious and harmonious development.

The yearning of some has already precipitated the descent of the Supermind, and now that it is an active principle in Earth-atmosphere it will go about its task of pushing up the covered Supermind from within the matrix of Matter. It will seize the structures of mind-life-matter and remold those that are cooperative to make active here in our very breath and minutest activity of life the Joy at the very heart of life. We shall be pushed to become one with our inevitable and irresistible golden future.

DYNAMIZATION OF A SYNTHESIZED WORLD CURRENT

India and USA stand on opposite sides of the globe. This is no accident. India is the ancient center for a spiritual-approach to life. USA is the modern center for a materialistic-approach to life. Throughout Earth's history, regions in geographic proximity to these centers have tended to display approaches in consonance with the neighboring center. Thus, Southeast Asia and Africa possess cultures where there is a strong emphasis on what the eye cannot see. European countries on the other hand, possess cultures where there is a predominantly materialistic outlook to life.

These centers are situated as far away as possible from each other and can be viewed as two ends of a global pole or global battery or power source which have through history been the foci from which powerful Earth-developing currents have emanated. In the last few centuries the West has been the source for much of Earth's development. Thus, materialistic progress has dominated and today myriad properties of Matter have been harnessed to provide for countless conveniences and comforts which have spread themselves evenly across the globe.

At the same time there has been a build up of problems on every level of life. It is clear that a materialistic approach to life is inadequate in solving these problems, and in fact has been responsible, through an approach of isolated development without regard to the deeper needs of humanity, for many problems we are faced with today. The deeper needs of humanity, the province of the unseen, the province of Wisdom, has to be met with less resistance so that a harmonic and many-sided development becomes the norm in all future endeavors.

To this effect the ancient center of the East, which has always remained alive, and which has always been releasing its currents of wisdom has to be actively turned to and dynamized. The dynamization will occur through the awakening of politics and the awakening of business, the primary strongholds of resistance, to the inner realities of being. In that India has been the center of the Spirit, and in that today it possesses a concentration of every conceivable world-problem within its boundaries, the awakening of both politics and business to this deeper reality would have most impact if experienced here.

Once the Eastern pole has been sufficiently stimulated through this build-up of charge, the ever-living current will then grow in puissance to sweep across the globe just as the current of Materialism swept across the globe to forge the realities of today. The diametrically-opposed centers will act to draw and strengthen this global current until the domains of Matter and Spirit have been overtly harmonized to thereby usher in an age of global coordination and wisdom.

The political awakening

Politicians are the choice of people and as such are an index of the thought and will active in Society. When politicians of their own free-choice turn to the Spirit, it will be an indication that the people have turned to the Spirit, and that the Nation has begun to overtly align with the deeper intent of Nature. This overt alignment represents the demand on India in the interest of World-development.

India has come full circle and is in the midst now of a formidable battle. Centuries ago she had opened her gates to the British, had been utterly subdued by them, and only with the birth of beings such as Rammohan Roy, Dayanand, Bankim Chandra, Ramakrishna, Bal Gangadhar Tilak, Vivekananda, and Sri Aurobindo, rose again through the fire of their tapasya into a nation flaming with cries and the final reality of Independence. India faces again a battle which demands every bit of courage that was possessed by those formidable and God-inspired beings. Her battle, as some politicians would have us believe, is not against the British or any other foreign power, but against her very own flesh and blood, her very own children, who have become enamored of personal power and wealth and forget what it is to be Indian.

As a people Indians have been ground into the dust and plundered for centuries. No wonder they have lost all self-esteem, pride of their heritage, and ability to stand like men. Instead, they have emulated without question the practices and ideologies of the West and even in this day and age, after having received those flaming pioneers into the heart of the country, look admirably and with a sense of wonder toward the Western nations. But those flaming pioneers did not come in vain. They ignited the fire of Indian Nationalism, taught many to recognize the Truth of their being, the secret Deity in each and every heart, and to seek guidance from there alone, so that the growing Godhead may spread its presence and manifest itself through conscious beings to finally uplift the entire human race. They had thus sown the seeds which will culminate in the releasing of India's active current and a relative subsiding of the current of materialization.

Politics today is a game of corruption and deceit. It is the child of petty satisfactions and not, as it should be, the midwife of the ever emerging Godhead. Politicians grab votes by instigating religious differences. Most of these politicians think of themselves as Nationalist. Yet they have not the slightest idea of what it means to be a Nationalist. A Nationalist is one whose only aim is the victory and government of the Great Mother. A Nationalist is one whose country comes first, and self second. A Nationalist is one who is willing and able without any qualm, to throw himself into the national fire of aspiration. A Nationalist is one who has recognized the true mission of India and is not willing to desecrate or compromise her spirit in any way. A Nationalist is one who through self-sacrifice builds up the charge needed to stimulate this Eastern power source.

The spirit of India is the spirit of unity through diversity. It is the spirit of all that is noble, heroic and divine. An utter inconsistency and sheer misunderstanding of this spirit is being displayed by many of today's politicians and parties. Parties, for example, are clamoring for Muslim, Christian or Hindu vote. Yet, being Hindu for example, means having a respect, understanding, and openness towards every other religion. For is not God infinite? And are not the number of faces and ways He shows us also infinite? What then gives one of his faces precedence over another?

Hinduism is a Dharma and a universal way of being in which all religions and viewpoints meet and combine to form a more dynamic and living synthesis. To cast one community against another is the play of ignorant individuals who are motivated by entirely selfish and un-Indian motives and spirit. India will not be ruled by this creed. These parties may continue to win elections in these times, but it will be only to sift out this strain from the rest of the Indians. It will be only so that all other Indians become aware of this coterie of Indians who would slay their own Mother to fulfill their petty aims and personal satisfactions. If this attitude has prevailed thus far it is only so that the eastern currents of spirituality may remain dormant while the western currents of materialization play their part in the overall development of the world. But now that Materialization has spread itself globally it is time for the eastern currents to begin to manifest with equal vigor. We have therefore to even thank these individuals for playing their parts so well in the overall scheme of things. For apart from keeping the natural currents of India suppressed, they are performing too the work of churning to separate the chaff from the wheat. By calling attention on their motives, selves, and pylons of misrule, they are preparing the rest of India to develop the strength and nobility to finally overcome them.

There has also been a movement by some parties and politicians to blindly turn away foreign companies who are investing in India. When the British ruled India it was necessary to boycott their goods and instead develop indigenous industry because the British had no intention of developing India for India's sake, but developing her in only those narrow paths that would lead to Britain's own commercial enrichment. Today, however, Indians control India. The threat therefore, of foreign commercialism exploiting India is invalid. The government can and has laid down stipulations demanding that foreign companies develop Indian infrastructure, hire locally, use local suppliers and distribution channels, in conducting their business. The result of such stipulations is that local employment rises, local wages increase, local infrastructure develops either because foreigners apply pressure on the government so that they may operate in conditions more like in their home countries, or they develop it themselves. Vaster amounts of money are released and used for the needed development of the local people and environment. Where this does not happen, there the government needs to apply the necessary policies to ensure that it does. In general, everyone has something to gain from foreign investment. The foreign companies manufacture their product, most likely, at a lower cost, and find an immediate market comprised of India's burgeoning middle class. The middle class now have a wider range of product to choose from at a more affordable rate. Local people develop their talents in different ways through working for corporations in capacities they may not have worked in before, and India as a whole engages in an active and living dialogue with the rest of the world, imbibing therefore its manifold impulses while her own spirit simultaneously begins to spread abroad. Further, the entry of foreign companies would instigate competition and force Indian companies to operate on world standards. There is enough money, power, knowledge, and ability in India that every kind of venture imaginable can be undertaken and become successful if it is conducted in the right spirit.

Policies to blindly suppress foreign investment, and policies to seek votes from chosen communities only, are detrimental to the long-term health of India and can be seen as being active only to keep India's spiritual fire toned down, so that Materialization may reach a peak in its crusade across the World. But the development of the World demands that India's indigenous fires be freely released, and therefore such policies and such politicians who promote them must of necessity diminish in force and occurrence.

The doors of India have opened now so that India may once again receive all the world impulses and synthesize it into her great spirit. India has existed for millennia. Centuries ago aspects of her being went forth into the world and developed entire countries in the East and West. The aspect of unity, for instance, traveled from India to the West, was resurrected in Christianity, and resulted in the formation of Christian nations. Through the ages these very countries then cast their gaze back toward India and knocked again at her doors. Some forcibly entered her and thought themselves her rulers. Providence had made her conquest possible so that under the guise of being her leader they may again receive some impulse to guide them through the following centuries. In this day and age India receives again from the World. Those forms, manifest now as multinational corporations, seek again to return into the Ocean of creativity to be assimilated, greatened, and cast forth again in some other, diviner mold.

India is not for India's sake alone, but for the World's. Her indigenous industries must become world class, just as all her other powers must, and that is not going to happen under this misguided protectionism being preached by her short-sighted, vote-seeking politicians. Policies to banish Muslims from some parts of the country, to attack Hindu pilgrims in another, to abort much needed infrastructure development, to form purposeless power-seeking coalitions, to cast out world-class companies, are motivated by personal reasons and will be looked back as nothing more than the actions of a few who are destined to become extinct, in the annals of history. Of necessity another group will rise. These will be the people sickened by the continued misrule and petty motives of today's leaders. These will be the children of God who follow no other impulsion than the voice of the Mother. These will be the keepers of the Spirit who shall unleash its life-giving current so that it may flow unrestricted to the other pole. These will be the modern Rishis whose very meaning will be to carry out the Divine decree and manifest here in matter, the life divine.

The business awakening

Whilst a political awakening reflects that people have awoken to the reality of the Spirit, a business awakening implies that people have actively begun to dynamize that

Spirit across all quarters of life. With the awakening of business to this reality the final stronghold of resistance is offered up to unleash, finally, the fires of the Spirit.

The last few years has seen a turnaround in the Indian economy. After independence the leaders of the nation made a decision to build a socialistic India. Given the fact that the British had done nothing to develop indigenous industry, and that India's primary economic activity was to supply raw materials and cheap labor to the British, this was the needed decision. Over the next few decades economic activity was more or less controlled by the government who issued licenses, set quotas, limited foreign corporate entry and investment, controlled imports and exports, and taxed excessively. Whilst these practices were essential in building the infrastructure and reorienting India towards indigenous economic activity, it also gave those who controlled it, namely the politicians and bureaucrats, excessive power and its consequent incentive to continue with the existing socialistic structure, despite signs and signals to the contrary. Thus, all attempts to alter the structure to allow freer economic activity and accelerate the growth of much needed infrastructure was met with resistance and downright opposition. In 1991 however, India's economic situation was so dismal, with economic growth of only 0.9 per cent, a virtual stagnation of industrial production, external debt growing at the rate of US$ 8 billion per year, and foreign currency reserves of less than US$ 1 billion, that even the politicians and bureaucrats had to pay attention, and begin to do something about it.

The corruption and vested interests of the few in lieu of

the many had finally cast its net of inertia across the machinery of Indian economic activity, and ground it to an almost complete halt. The very soul of India had rebelled against the torpor and ignorant rule of her children, and pulled in attention from world agencies such as the IMF, to ignite the dying economy with an imposed program of reforms. This signalled the peak of India's lethargy and inertia, and the last movement in a cycle which now has yielded to a cycle of growth and outward-focused movement. Thus began the economic reform process in India.

Economic liberalization began with the almost complete removal of the licensing system. Domestic companies could now compete in a number of key sectors without obtaining licenses from the affiliated bureaucrats and politicians. Customs duties were reduced to thereby make international and more economically-produced domestic goods available. The consumer now had a wider and more affordable selection of goods to choose from. Tax levels were reduced thereby providing greater incentive to businesses and individuals to report correctly. This increased the revenues of the government. Further, businesses now had an incentive to produce more since they could retain more of the revenues they had earned. Foreign investment and collaboration were welcomed thus providing business people with additional capital flows to select from. Access to a plethora of foreign technologies also became economically feasible. Finally, foreign collaboration offered a chance to Indian companies to compete on a global level using the venture as a conduit into foreign markets. India had allowed her gates to be opened to the world economy.

Capital from all over the world began to flow into India to revitalize the age-old instincts for economic activity and adventure. The chains that burdened and contained the entrepreneurial instincts of her people were finally removed. The result has been encouraging. Where most countries have experienced a further slow-down in economic activity during the reform process, because of the uncertainty of where the reform process may be headed, India has shown a continuous growth across many of the key economic indicators.

India is destined to be amongst the leaders of the world. For whenever Earth is to enter a period of harmony and fulfillment, then the World Teacher must arise and take her place in the march of nations, and pour her knowledge into the world. The Eastern pole of the global battery must play its part in the flow of power. The current of spirituality with its deep wisdom and comprehensive and all-encompassing outlook must flow freely so that all is united and begins to travel forward as a beautifully diverse whole.

It is at this critical time that a demand must be made on the businessperson of India. India possesses a wealth of knowledge. It is a nation thousands of years old, fashioned and shaped by the tapasya and effulgence of her Rishis. These superhumans turned their gaze within and through tapasya discovered the beauty of the inner life. They transcended all obstacles and in the process discovered the secrets of human psychology and human existence. Their effulgence caused them to create a harmony between the inner and outer, and they gifted India with many precious systems that form the visible kernel of her inner spirit. They mapped out the intricacies of the human constitution, the many parts of the being, the intention, nature, and purpose of the parts, and the secrets and hidden destiny which each contained behind its many veils. They discovered the intentions and secrets of nature, and lived intimately with the Rhythm from which all life emerges and which informs, sustains, and surrounds all life. They saw in each rose, in each cloud and stream and rising tree, the smile and substance of He who is master and player of this increasingly complex and beautiful game. They saw the infinite variety in life and were the overt architects of a social system whose liberalism was the underlying theme, and whose fulfillment of variety by the natural law and nature of each, the stride that led to harmony. Century after century the kernel of India's spirit exposed itself through the seekings of the Rishis. Music, architecture, literature, and drama became avenues to manifest and express that kernel, and the very soul of India and her many-sided and intricate vibration and intent became a natural part of everyone's life.

The spirit that creates and manifests as beauty wove itself into the fabric of society. It spread far and wide, across the corners of India, and its beauty and its knowledge and its teachership became the essence and the natural substance of the very material of India. This magnificence has expressed itself in myriad forms. The Vedas, the Upanishads, the Mahabharatha, and the Ramayana are examples of its insightful and life-encompassing literature. Her splendid temples and palaces vast in form and arising like fires and subtleties of stone expressing their aspiration for eternal beauty, are examples of her architecture. Her song and instrumental masterpieces which elevates a listener to unnatural heights and inner depths and exerts a constant pressure on the inner doors which finally open to release one into the vastness of a wider self, are examples of her music. Her system of Ayurveda with its holistic approach and balance of the many parts of the being with the individual habits, seasons, and sway of society, is an example of her enlightened system of maintaining health. Her vast and tremendous insight into the whole dynamism of the human, and the dynamism of society, with their corresponding shastras, enlightened laws, and swabhavas, natures, are examples of her enlightened administration.

It is this spirit of assimilative creativity, made manifest through the Rishis of past, which must break through the imprisoning realities of the business environment so that even organizations and companies may become triumphant expressions of the Infinite. It is this spirit which must be inculcated by each employee in each company so that he may become creative as the Rishi was creative. It is this spirit which of necessity must sweep across the world so that her development may become harmonic and many-sided. It is thus inevitable that India, and her businesses, must rise.

The opening of India's gates to the global economy has ushered in a vast and growing number of multinational companies, and a vast and growing number of joint collaborations and ventures across the spectrum of industries. Now a host of Indian companies have the opportunity through these ventures and the opening up of the economy, to thrust themselves into the global battlefield of commerce and activity, and emerge as world-players. The very spread of Materialism, emanating from the pole at the West toward the East, has opened the doors for Spirituality, its complementary and fulfilling current, to emanate from the pole at the East towards the West.

It has been the practice, and understandably so, of companies all over the world to emulate companies who are global leaders. The realities of the global marketplace have tempered and fashioned the practices of the leading corporations, and many excellent practices have emerged. These practices include detailed financial analyses such as 'cash-flow' and 'return on investment' analysis. They include the direction-forming 'strategic planning' practice, the market and company core-competency matching 'market planning' practice, the thorough process-driven 'activity based costing' practice, and the innovative and habit breaking practice of 'reengineering'. These practices have enabled companies to become globally competitive and are indispensable to the efficient and effective functioning of a successful company. These practices are manifestations of the materialistic approach to life, and while absolutely necessary, must of necessity be balanced by practices which are manifestations of the spiritual approach to life. It is not surprising therefore to find that on other fronts even these global companies are lacking. Namely, in the areas of people and team management. Inevitably, a majority of team efforts become a clash of egos and a battle of personal opinions not quite based on the total picture. Further, companies may have the intention of changing the way they currently operate, may effectively plan out at a macro-level what needs to be done, but then fail effectively to execute the details at the implementation level. For example, with the potential productivity improvements of wide-scale automation many companies computerized their internal operations. Yet, few if any have actualized the predicted levels of efficiency and productivity. Why? Another company, for example, was required to change its strategic direction because of the threat of competition. It excellently visualized and planned the macro-level changes that had to take place. Yet when it came down to implementation and when the behaviors and habits of the employees performing the tasks had to change to really make the endeavor successful, the effort failed and realized only a shadow of its original intention.

Thus, while the financial, strategic, accounting, and marketing systems have been honed to perfection and provide excellent instrumentation in providing a company with the wherewithal to maneuver through the increasingly complex global environment, the human systems, the view of humans, the way they interact, and an understanding of who they are, is a fledgling practice and remains poor and ill-understood at best. Human issues are in fact the strength of the Indian Spirit. For human assets are none other than the embodiment of the omnipresent Spirit. The age-old teachings of India must be revisited for their insight into human beings, and for their profound knowledge of creativity, human interaction, and the organic development of groups. The demand on the businessperson of India is to tap into the Spirit of India to complete the barrage of instrumentation and knowledge needed to assure that business teams and employers learn to effectively coordinate and develop their human assets. Then only will the balance inherent in the range of possibilities on the East-West spectrum have been correctly mobilized.

Conclusion

The awakening of the political and business worlds to the realities of the inner being will make active an important spiritual impetus so that a harmonized material-spiritual outlook and way of life can become the norm in all daily activities. The already flowing current of spirituality having thus penetrated the strongholds of resistance, shall then emanate with added vigor and subsume the flow of materiality within it. The resulting synthesized world current will cause problems to be looked at anew from a deeper point of view, and cause all future endeavors to be undertaken in a more harmonic fashion. An era of harmonized development will thus have been ushered in.